Those were the 50s

Steve Pope

SIMON & SCHUSTER
A VIACOM COMPANY

First published in Great Britain by Simon & Schuster UK Ltd, 2003
A Viacom Company

Simon & Schuster UK Ltd
Africa House
64–78 Kingsway
London
WC2B 6AH

1 3 5 7 9 10 8 6 4 2

Design: Clare Sleven
Typesetting: Stylize Digital Artwork Ltd
Printed and bound in China
ISBN 0 74324 844 9

Picture credits
All photos are © Hulton Getty with the following exceptions:
The Advertising Archive: 30, 34, 44, 51, 90, 100.
Empics: 43.
John Frost Newspapers: 41.
NASA: 86.
Ronald Grant Archive: 27, 31, 39, 53.

Contents

Introduction

Popular history hasn't been good to the 50s. Sandwiched between the Second World War and the Swinging 60s, like dry bread inside two pieces of meat, they've been pigeon-holed as dull and all but ignored.

Weighed against the high triumphs and disasters of the War years, the 50s have been dismissed as a tense, uncertain postscript. Seen through the haze of a beat generation's wild and crazy flowerings, they look like a pinched, monochrome preamble. All in all, they're a bit of a grey area, and posterity prefers nice, simple labels.

So while the War and the 60s won't leave us alone, the 50s are becoming quite hard to find. We are drowning in pop histories, documentaries, Top Tens and every imaginable heritage-related product – but not about the 50s. While almost any reader or viewer can name dozens of famous people, places and events from the exciting times either side, most 50s landmarks have been left in peace. Take away Elvis, whose image-peddlers could teach the Vatican a thing or two about heritage marketing, and anyone who wasn't there could be forgiven for jumping straight to Kennedy or the Beatles.

Hovering between a glorious past and an exciting future – illuminations in London's Battersea Park for the 1951 Festival of Britain summed up the uncertainties of the early 50s.

Popular history is missing something. The decade that gave birth to modern lifestyles was crammed with social upheavals and innovations, heaving with landmark events and personalities, and alive with the shock of the new. Science was tooling up to finally conquer nature, and the wider world was in the grip of one long, shuddering geopolitical earthquake. Life in the 50s was an accelerating rollercoaster hurtling towards a future of seemingly limitless horizons, shadowed all the way by the unprecedented and terrifying spectre of total nuclear destruction.

All that, and Lonnie Donegan too... bring on the 1950s!

Youth culture and mass consumerism – pipedreams in 1950 – were facts of life by 1957, when skiffle king Lonnie Donegan and his group starred in this early edition of *Six-Five Special*, British TV's first pop show.

At least posterity has left the 50s intact. Its intense spotlight on the War has cut the 40s in half, leaving them with a relatively uncharted dark side. So what happened to Britain in the late 40s? In a sentence, they were a period of recovery, scene setting and profound national shock.

The War took some getting over. For a time, as people slowly got out of uniform, the country was 'demob happy', cheerfully clearing away the damage and celebrating survival, but the picture didn't look too rosy once the novelty wore off. The Labour Party had been elected in 1945 on a tide of good intentions and determination to build a better future out of the rubble. With a bankrupt nation reduced to dependence on US aid, world trade in chaos and the Empire proving a lot more troublesome than helpful, Britons found themselves toiling, for little immediate reward, to finance a welfare state and an ambitious nationalisation programme.

Political reputations would soon depend on radio and television, but for now they were still built on personal oratory, a set of wheels and a loudspeaker. Michael Foot, about to enter parliament for the first time, would nevertheless remain first and foremost a public speaker throughout a distinguished political career.

While Britain was patching itself up, the rest of the world seemed to be leaving it behind. India finally won independence in 1947, and much of the old Empire was redefined as the Commonwealth in 1949. By that time the planet had been taken over by two superpowers, Russia and America, with newly Communist China being touted as a possible third, and they were remaking the world in their own image. The phrase 'Cold War' had passed from American journalism into popular usage in 1947, just as the 'Truman Doctrine' was announcing America's intention to police the world against Communism. Not long ago, Britain had been the world's policeman, and it would be a long time before the country got used to being a mere deputy.

Superpowers apart, most countries were poor and relatively powerless in the late 40s, but even broken Germany and proud, enfeebled France came out of the shock more quickly than Britain. Psychologically speaking, it isn't hard to guess why. To the average British mind the entire history of the nation had been one long procession towards, and fulfilment of, greatness – until now.

Keep Taking the Medicine

As Britain celebrated its fifth new year since the peace, most of the nation's energies were still focused on getting over the War. The world was in the midst of a giant shake-up, but Britain seemed to be watching from the sidelines, and while Americans in particular marched confidently towards an 'affluent' society, Britain was lagging behind, stuck in a dreary post-War hangover by the name of 'austerity'.

Spoils of War

Apart from basic survival and full employment – a blessing shared by most nations during post-war reconstruction – what had Britain got for winning the War? In the absence of old-fashioned rewards, such as riches or territories, the big prize on offer was Labour's ambitious welfare state programme, but the NHS was still under construction in 1950, and social security from 'cradle to grave' was still more promise than practice. In the meantime, the fruits of victory amounted to little more than hard work and poverty.

Everyday conditions were actually more stringent than those in wartime. Every citizen had to carry an identity card, while rationing still applied to petrol, sweets, tea, sugar, butter and cheese. All meat was rationed – four ounces per week for bacon, and about three ration books for a steak – and much else was often impossible to come by. Labour shortages at home and trade weakness aboard meant that tobacco, steel, coal and many imported consumer goods could all be hard to find.

If you wanted to push the boat out and have a good time, Clement Attlee's government was quite deliberately making it difficult. Fired by the intense rhetoric of health minister Aneurin (Nye) Bevan, Labour was imposing austerity for the common good, a campaign personified by Chancellor Sir Stafford Cripps, a man whose lifestyle and appearance chimed perfectly with his role as the nation's conscience and taxman.

Cripps had imposed purchase and entertainment taxes on everything from toys to cinema tickets, and basic income tax stood at 9s 6d in the pound (47.5 percent), rising sharply to a maximum of 15s (75 percent). Not that high tax brackets mattered to most people. The average weekly wage stood at £6. 8s (£6.40), and the Inland Revenue were only aware of 70 people whose annual salary amounted to more than £6,000. Even at a time when you could marry and set up home on an annual income of £300, the British hardly had money to burn. Just in case there was some spare cash, a price limit of five shillings (25 pence) was placed on any form of public entertainment, even a (relatively frugal) meal at the Ritz.

Prefabs, like these nestling in suburban Clapham, were the quick fix for Britain's desperate post-War housing shortage, and the new housing estate looming in the background was supposed to be the long-term solution. By the time they finally rendered prefabs redundant, in the 60s, housing estates were already failing.

The Last Hustings

An election was due in 1950, and called for on 23 February. The country's first winter election in modern times, it was also the last to be held without the involvement of television, which was only available to about 350,000 homes. Important politicians made occasional radio broadcasts, but personal appearances and oratory remained at the heart of electioneering.

As in 1945, the leaders of the main political parties were Clement Attlee and Winston Churchill. The latter was still a vote winner in his late seventies. They and other senior figures, such as foreign minister Ernest Bevin and his opposite number Anthony Eden, had worked together in the wartime coalition, and this was an essentially polite election, though Nye Bevan still slung a few gratuitous insults around.

The abolition of double votes for business owners and separate seats for the oldest universities helped Labour, but boundary commission constituency changes and, above all, the introduction of postal voting were bigger plusses for the opposition. Labour's attempts to woo electors by raising the sweet and bacon rations also backfired when West Germany announced the imminent abolition of rationing on everything except sugar. With nationalisation emerging as the election's central issue, and signs that Labour was losing support in the more prosperous southeast, the campaign seemed be to swinging towards Churchill's Conservatives.

The vote itself was very different from today's televised extravaganzas. For one thing, a record 84 percent of voters turned out. For another, it took two days for

the results to be gathered and a winner to emerge. After one day, it looked like another Labour landslide but, once the rural and postal votes were counted, Attlee's government was returned to power with a slender overall majority of five seats. It was hardly a decisive mandate, or a recipe for efficient government, and a rematch was certain in the near future. The only definite decision to emerge from the result, apart from the dismal failure of 100 Communist candidates, saw the Liberals consigned to near oblivion, winning only nine seats and losing 319 deposits.

Chancellor Sir Stafford Cripps pushes the boat out, treating himself to a cup of tea, half a smile and a bun. No jam, of course...

Spy Fever

There has probably never been a conspiracy theory like it, and there may never be again. A gigantic web of sedition was being woven by legions of Communist spies in the midst of democratic societies, and especially in America, where they were poised close to the very centre of power. An obscure Republican senator, Joe McCarthy of Wisconsin, made this message his own in 1950, and then made it an American national obsession.

It had begun in the late 40s. As the Cold War took hold of hearts and minds, Congress looked to expose Communists and ex-Communists, or 'Reds', as potential traitors. Its eyes and ears were the FBI and the CIA, both deeply committed to the idea of a conspiracy. Its court of inquisition was the House Un-American Activities Committee (HUAC), where public interviews with suspects transmitted the fear to ordinary Americans.

The arrest in 1949 of a State Department insider, Alger Hiss, made the Red Peril seem a lot more credible. His conviction for passing secret documents to the USSR in the 1930s, secured on flimsy hearsay evidence, made the name of his chief Senate accuser, future President Richard Nixon, and alerted America to the possibility of treachery at the top.

The gleam of history in his eyes, the press hanging on his every word, every word feeding fear into American hearts and minds. Joe McCarthy in his prime.

The new decade opened with an even bigger shock to America's sense of security, this time from over here. On 25 January, the chief physicist at the UK's Harwell nuclear research centre, Klaus Fuchs, was arrested as a spy on evidence supplied by the FBI.

Unlike so many accused in his wake, Fuchs was the real thing. He had worked on the first atomic weapons at Los Alamos and had willingly supplied the USSR with all he knew about nuclear energy. Fuchs got 14 years, though he served only nine, and a furious United States slapped a ban on the release of nuclear secrets to Britain.

Enter Joe McCarthy. McCarthy caused a sensation with a speech on 9 February, when he claimed to know the names of 205 active Communists 'still working and shaping policy in the State Department'. The enormous impact of these unproven accusations was promptly multiplied by the FBI, which revealed that Klaus Fuchs had an American contact, Harry Gold, whose spy network included a husband and wife team, Julius and Ethel Rosenberg. Spy fever and McCarthy were suddenly unstoppable.

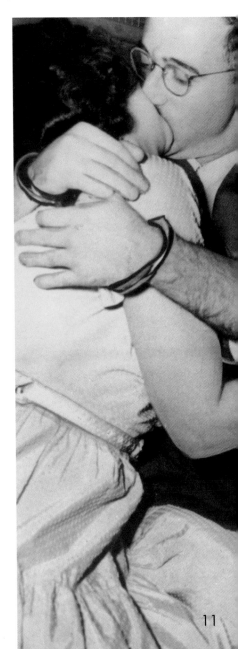

The evidence, or lack of it, against the Rosenbergs, who were eventually executed in June 1953, reminded more than one commentator of a mediaeval witch-hunt. The parallel would soon become abundantly clear as McCarthy and a growing band of fellow travellers made a grim, international catchphrase of the question: 'Are you now, or have you ever been, a Communist?'

Movers and Shakers

Cooler heads than Joe McCarthy or rabidly anti-Communist FBI chief Edgar Hoover were worrying about the realities behind the Reds scare. The arrest of Fuchs persuaded US President Harry Truman to override ethical doubts among his own scientific advisors, and four days later he authorised urgent development of a new hydrogen bomb, or H-Bomb. Once the USSR confirmed its own possession of an atomic bomb, in March, the nuclear arms race was public knowledge. Ignorance would have been more reassuring in a world that was looking dangerously volatile. Newly independent India and Pakistan, the Israeli state just planted in Palestine, Soviet-controlled Eastern Europe, Communist China... all these and

Are they heartless traitors, motivated by greed, or tragic scapegoats for a frightened FBI? Julius and Ethel Rosenberg have just been arraigned for treason, on verbal evidence provided by unreliable witnesses. Handcuffed, they kiss on their way to prison.

more seemed likely to destabilise a global peace that still felt precarious. Meanwhile America had just become fully involved in the war-torn French colony of Vietnam, promising to protect the south against Communist attack, but it was another promise of protection, this time by the United Nations as a whole to South Korea, that went critical in 1950.

On 25 June, Communist North Korea invaded south across the 38th Parallel frontier, which had only been evacuated by US forces in 1949. Assuming, wrongly it seems, that the Russians were involved, Truman rushed a United Nations resolution into force during a Soviet boycott of the security council, and troops from occupied Japan were back in Korea by the end of the month. Hopelessly outnumbered, they could only retreat until reinforcements, including British and other UN contingents, arrived in September. Beefed up UN forces under Douglas MacArthur drove a counter-offensive back into North Korea by October, at which point the Chinese intervened on behalf of North Korea, halting UN progress with massive, if ill-equipped, armies.

The year ended in military stalemate, but with Chinese forces building dangerously and MacArthur sounding even more dangerous. Nothing if not aggressive, and certainly no diplomat, the old war hero made it publicly clear in December that nuclear weapons were his preferred option in Korea. MacArthur hadn't asked his commander-in-chief's permission for this outburst, and while Britain edged towards Christmas wondering about a third world war, Harry Truman was deciding he'd had enough of mavericks.

Western Approaches
The British public was agog with fascination at 'Reds Under The Beds' in Washington, but a sense of superior grace under pressure didn't stop us gobbling up American culture.

Home-grown war movies and comedies did well in Britain, where Jack Lee's *The Wooden Horse* was the year's fourth most popular film, but Hollywood's influence over the global movie business was as powerful as ever. The box office champions were Disney's *Cinderella* and the dark pairing of William Holden with comeback queen Gloria Swanson in *Sunset Boulevard*. Bette Davis in *All About Eve* took the Oscar honours, while *Harvey*, *Father of the Bride* and *The Men*, with Marlon Brando, all enjoyed worldwide success.

America had always led the world in movie making, but now it seemed to dominate every strand of modern culture. The world's hottest author was undoubtedly the action-packed American Ernest Hemingway, whose *Across the River and Into the Trees* was one of the year's big publishing events. Americans, headed by Isaac Asimov and Robert A Heinlein, also dominated an explosion of new science fiction writing, in magazines and novels, which became standard fare for a generation of British schoolboys.

In the world of fine arts, the undoubted fame of Pablo Picasso and an elderly Henri Matisse was being outshone by Wyoming backwoods recluse Jackson Pollock, whose spidery, apparently random creations ushered a prolific generation of American 'action painters' into the artistic mainstream. Even architecture's big event of 1950 took place in America, where the huge, glass-sided box of the New York United Nations building joined a skyline still dominated by the Art Deco whimsies of pre-war big business.

Island Life

Much more attention was paid to local and schools sport than it is today, but the calendar of great national events was well established. The Football League, won by Portsmouth for the second year running, was still drawing huge post-War crowds, as was the first division in Scotland, where Rangers won the double. The FA Cup final, a 2-0 win for Arsenal over Liverpool,

The weekly *Picture Post* was a national institution by 1950, attracting half a million readers with a mix of powerful photo-spreads and lively reportage. It also had a knack for catching the mood of the day, nicely summed up that autumn by this US tank commander's anxious vigilance in Korea.

13

was still considered the most important match in the world. Although England sent a team to that summer's World Cup finals for the first time, its disastrous fate at a chaotic tournament in Brazil – elimination after an ignominious 1-0 defeat by, of all people, the USA – was shrugged off as an unfortunate triviality in the middle of the cricket season. Quite a cricket season it was too, as the West Indies came to England and smashed the illusion that Australia were the home nation's only really worthy opponents.

The brilliance of Ramadhin, Valentine, Worrall, Woolcott and Weekes was part of a trend that would soon erode the country's sporting pride. Americans and Australians dominated the first half of the decade at Wimbledon, where generations of local hand-wringing were already well underway, and they were already undisputed masters of international golf. Crowds that flocked to the world's first grand prix event at Silverstone in May – won by Italian Nino Farina in an Alfa Romeo – would also get used to regular doses of British failure. No British cars and only one British driver, Reg Parnell, finished in the top fifteen of the 1950 championship, and the sport's first years were dominated by the brilliant Argentine, Juan-Manuel Fangio.

Man of the Hour
Everything about Sir Stafford Cripps could have been designed as a, somewhat eccentric, model for the austere life he

Big Box

Designed by a particularly acrimonious committee, the gigantic box of the UN Building was completed in 1950 and opened the following year. Regarded then as one of the wonders of the modern world, it exerted a massive influence over future building, in Britain as well as America. Imitations of what became known as 'corporate' style did not appear at once in London, but the Shell Building was completed on the South Bank in 1958, setting a local trend soon followed by Castrol House in Marylebone, Bowater House in Knightsbridge and Thorn House in the West End. The UN Building's modernist simplicity was taken to greater heights in New York by Lever House in 1952 and the Seagram Building in 1958. It has since been dismissed as a good idea gone wrong, and blamed for architecture's subsequent obsession with functional box-structures in functional concrete.

recommended to the nation. An academic, a devout Christian and a vegetarian, he sought a world dominated by moral rather than material concerns and appeared to have no vices at all. Credited with the gloomy phrase 'no jam today', he was known as the nation's 'thorn of conscience' as he tried to rebuild a shattered, debt-ridden economy with low consumer spending and high taxes. Though Cripps was never a vote catcher, his resignation through illness at the end of the year was a blow to the weakened Labour government. His subsequent death from cancer robbed the Party of a dedicated and effective administrator.

Shining Star

Television was still a social irrelevance in Britain, but was already becoming a major industry in the United States, where the number of sets in use shot up from 1.5 million to 15 million in a year. Though big American film and stage stars still avoided the new medium, it was starting to create national and international stars of its own. None shone brighter than the sequinned vision that was Liberace, American music's first great TV star. First seen by viewers in 1950, he turned purest schmaltz into money, talking lovingly to audiences and dazzling them with his grin, if not his musical talents. Critics hated him, of course, but his cheerful reaction to well-earned public ridicule – 'I cried all the way to the bank' – became an international catchphrase for consumerism.

OTHER NEWS...

... submarine *HMS Truculent* collides with a Danish tanker in the Thames Estuary, and sinks, killing 60 people... India formally becomes a republic on 26 January... American business gives the world the electric typewriter, self-opening lifts, the first credit cards and the xerox machine... antihistamines catch on.... world population is about 2.3 billion... 1.5 million Germans have been missing since 1945... Chancellor Cripps predicts budget surplus... 480 million of the world's 800 million children are undernourished... world's worst air crash kills 80 at Sigginston, Wales, in March... major earthquake strikes Assam... Chiang Kai-Shek returns as President of 'Nationalist China'... the 'Hollywood Ten' are jailed for contempt of Congress while under investigation as suspected Communists... London dock strike in April, troops later deployed to unload ships... Dylan Thomas storms the USA with a first reading tour... Uruguay wins the first post-War world cup... UK petrol rationing ends in May... Anglo-Egyptian agreement rescheduling troop removals... Britain and the US recognise the Vietnamese government of emperor Bao Dai... William Cooper's *Tales from Provincial Life*... soap rationing ends in September... Labour conference decides to nationalise iron and steel industries... Indonesia becomes a member of the UN on 28 September.... *The Lion, the Witch and the Wardrobe*, written by CS Lewis... the world's longest pipeline, at 1,068 miles, is completed in the Lebanon... war drama *Odette* is a big British box office hit... sci-fi classics of 1950: Isaac Asimov's *I, Robot*, Ray Bradbury's *The Martian Chronicles*, Robert A. Heinlein's *The Man Who Sold the Moon*... China invades Tibet in October... Charles Schultz publishes the first Peanuts cartoon... British cinemas sell 1,400 million tickets in 1950... Marshall Plan aid to Britain will end in the New Year... at Christmas, Scottish Nationalist pranksters steal the Stone of Destiny from Westminster Abbey; it is later recovered from Arbroath Abbey.... goodbye: Edgar Rice Burroughs, Al Jolson, Vaslav Nijinsky, George Orwell, George Bernard Shaw, Jan Smuts.

First light

All through a particularly wet and grey winter, the weather matched the world's mood. British troops were in Korea, and American 'hawks' were talking about a showdown with the Soviets. Austerity just wouldn't go away, despite abolition of the five shilling limit on 13 January, and home life still revolved around ration books, power cuts and shortages. Even traditionally British fare such as beef would be in short supply later in the year, once a trade dispute with Argentina began to bite.

Yet through those drab months a small but palpable sense of expectation was at large, above all in London but also in cities, towns and rural communities all over the country. For the first time since the War, the nation was about to have a party. People were actually being encouraged to enjoy themselves.

Opening day at the South Bank Festival site, and a chance to get down to some serious queuing outside its centrepiece, the Dome of Discovery. The site's architecture was usually described as 'futuristic' and, amazingly enough, a building much like the Dome would appear beside the Thames almost 50 years later.

Raindrop in the Desert

In the planning since 1948, with the enthusiastic approval of the royal family, the Festival of Britain was the big event of 1951. It ran from May to September, and though it cost £11 million to stage, a huge extravagance at the time, it was more of a brown ale knees-up than a champagne celebration. It was meant to be. Despite its echoes of the great 1851 Empire Exhibition, this festival was emphatically all about the faces of modern Britain.

There was no question of locating the Festival's centrepiece anywhere but London, still arguably the greatest city in the world. The site's exact location came down to a choice between the main 1851 site, Hyde Park, the wide open spaces of suburban Osterley Park, Battersea Park, and the eventual winner, the South Bank. The site's biggest selling points were good connections, and the LCC's existing plan to build the new Festival Hall on an adjacent plot.

Work began clearing a 27-acre patch of largely derelict, bomb-cratered riverside between Waterloo Station and County Hall. Construction fell steadily behind schedule, delayed by material shortages and a series of strikes, so that by the time it finally opened on 3 May, the whole event was being dismissed by cynics as an expensive muddle.

People liked the Skylon, they just weren't sure why. A temporary structure, due for demolition after the Festival, it could hardly be called a sculpture, but it didn't have a function and you couldn't go inside or climb it. Futuristic, though.

Yet despite the problems, the criticisms and the unfavourable comparisons with 1851, the Festival succeeded beyond anyone's expectations. More than 10 million people visited the South Bank site that summer, as the British public threw itself cheerfully into every celebration of modern Britishness the organisers could come up with.

The gaudy hotchpotch of bizarre, temporary structures that greeted visitors by the Thames wouldn't much impress modern consumers, but it worked in the entertainment desert of 1951. The main feature was the Dome of Discovery, a covered exhibition space something like the more recent Millennium Dome, but its most 'futuristic' vision was the Skylon, a huge stretched raindrop, with no actual purpose, that was held up by a complex series of cables. A set of pavilions showed off various aspects of British life – the home, school, industry, transport and the countryside – and there was even a defiantly modern pavilion devoted exclusively to design.

Towering carnival figures, open-air dancing, fountains and terraces, a giant chess set, sculptures by Moore, Sutherland and Epstein… the site was mayhem, with plenty of queuing and plenty of rain, but few complaints. Down the road at Battersea Pleasure Gardens, the Tree Walk and the miniature Oyster Railway were a must for kids of all ages, and younger children flocked to the Guinness clock as it struck the hour. Meanwhile London Transport made sure millions of visitors to London reached the site on brand new aluminium Tube trains.

Down Your Way

The Festival was always intended to be a national event, much more than just its London centrepiece, and at this level it was if anything even more successful. Six official exhibitions took place in major provincial cities, and two travelling exhibitions – one by land, and a smaller one aboard the Festival Ship *Campania* – toured condensed versions of the South Bank cultural pavilions, spending three weeks at a time in most of Britain's cities and ports. Another 50 or so exhibitions and arts festivals took place across the country, which was also awash with street parties, generally more boisterous than luxurious. More than 2,000 local authorities organised bigger events of their own, though it helped if morrismen were your cup of tea, and in all about 18 million people paid to visit them.

Red Perils

Korea still dominated the world's headlines. By the time peace talks began in July, the war had been through an offensive from the north and a UN counter-offensive, only to end up back at the frontier. The war also had to get by without Douglas MacArthur.

MacArthur had finally pushed Truman too far in late March, when he had sent the Chinese commander in Korea an ultimatum threatening nuclear attack. For Cold War 'hawks', most of them in America, his dismissal was a lost opportunity to strike at Communism while it was too weak to retaliate, and they treated MacArthur to a martyr's welcome on his return to the States. As the far right started calling Truman 'the Judas in the White House', and McCarthy claimed Communists were controlling the President, momentum gathered behind the unrepentant 70 year-old MacArthur as

There's a glint in the old fighter's eye as General Douglas MacArthur parades down Broadway to a tickertape welcome from the city of New York. His open desire to end the Cold War with nuclear weapons has cost him command in Korea, but seems to be playing pretty well back home.

his possible successor. Unfortunately for MacArthur, perhaps less so for the rest of the world, the Republican Party was already having doubts about McCarthy and wasn't ready to back another potentially unstable crusader. The old general made a strident TV broadcast backing demands for Truman's impeachment, but the call to political greatness never came.

Many celebrated Americans shared MacArthur's views. The opinions of actor John Wayne, who headed the Motion Picture Alliance for the Preservation of American Ideals, were already well known to his legions of fans, while fellow film star Ronald Reagan was particularly active in the exposure and banishment of Hollywood conspirators.

Red Faces
Korea's escalation to all-out nuclear conflict was still a frighteningly real possibility, especially after the United States had conducted its first, if less than completely successful, H-bomb test on 12 May. At this point, a new spy scandal was the last thing any one needed, especially the beleaguered British security services.

Donald Maclean and Guy Burgess, both diplomats with access to highly sensitive information, fled England on the night of 25 May, and British security's international reputation hit an all-time low. After the shock and humiliation of Klaus Fuchs, the sheer laxity that had allowed them to get away with treason was shocking, and the assumptions that lay behind it were even more so.

Maclean had well-known problems with drink and depression, as well as the habit of claiming to be a Russian spy when he'd had a few, but it hadn't damaged his career. He had been privy to American nuclear secrets, enjoyed the highest security clearance at the Atomic Energy Commission and become head of the Foreign Office American department in 1950. Guy Burgess was a heavy drinking, secretly homosexual member of the embassy staff in Washington, where he stayed with HAR 'Kim' Philby, Britain's liaison officer with the FBI and CIA. All three were spying for the Russians, but such Cambridge-educated 'gentlemen' were still considered above suspicion.

Donald Maclean – the intense-looking gent perched on the Washington ambassador's desk – never made much effort to blend in with the intelligence crowd. It didn't do his career any harm, but Churchill doesn't look too pleased about it.

When Maclean's years of espionage work finally looked like coming to light, Philby covered his own tracks by pointing the finger from Washington. Burgess got himself sent home in order to warn Maclean, and both were next seen on a Moscow newsreel in 1956. For British intelligence, soon to be immortalised in a wealth of spy fiction, treachery among the inner circle didn't quite provide the full wake-up call. Philby remained at large until the early 60s, bolstered by endorsements from some of the country's most respected figures, including Harold Macmillan.

Trademarks

Inventions were big news in the 1950s, because science and technology were on a roll. Boosted by crash wartime development programmes, and despite giving us The Bomb, they seemed to be on the verge of solving many of the most serious and persistent problems facing humanity as a whole.

Penicillin was in increasingly regular use throughout the developed world, and American scientist Max Theiler won the year's Nobel medicine prize for a new yellow fever vaccine. The combine harvester appeared in the US, as did commercial transistors and Univac, the first active business computer. Despite the menace of another new American product, the mighty B-52 bomber, even nuclear power revealed its positive side, when the first atomic electricity was generated at Acron, Ohio.

On a smaller scale, the year's great leap forward in fashion came from France, where Paris shoemaker Jordan invented the stiletto heel. The most leisure-friendly invention, the home tape recorder, came from Japan, which finally signed a peace treaty with the non-Communist wartime allies in September, ending six years of military occupation and heralding a new power on the international consumer markets.

Silly Boys

Despite producing a growing number of genuinely popular shows – *The Archers*, for instance, made its radio debut this year – the BBC had earned its reputation as a conservative, rather old-fashioned institution. It clearly didn't know quite what it was getting when it gave the go-ahead to a new comedy show called *Crazy People*. Better known by its revised name, *The*

Dock Days

London was the capital of state, Commonwealth and Empire, a financial and cultural centre, and a trading centre for the nations goods, but in the 1950s it remained first and foremost a port. Its docklands were crammed with merchant shipping from all over the globe, and the river area east of the City throbbed with activity and sound.

Foggy nights in town were still haunted by the moans of foghorns when the decade closed, but by then the docks were already in decline, and New York had taken over as the world's cultural capital. Though London would regain its cultural pre-eminence from time to time, the docks would be a fraction of their former size by the late 1970s.

Peter Sellers, Spike Milligan, Michael Bentine and Harry Secombe – The Goons address themselves to a telephone in 1951. With a little imagination, you can almost hear the silly voices.

Goon Show, the programme hit the airwaves in May and quickly took a grip on the nation's silly glands.

The ex-service humour of Michael Bentine, Harry Secombe, Peter Sellers and Spike Milligan owed debts to the Marx Brothers, Edward Lear and the surreal comedy of contemporary columnist JB Morton, or Beachcomber – but it soon evolved in its own right to become a very peculiar forum for British eccentricity. The BBC, driven to distraction by Goonish affronts to decency, good taste or the monarchy, made many efforts to stifle them, until an exasperated Spike Milligan finally gave up on the show in 1959.

Sensible Girls

The British film industry, which scored this year with *The Lavender Hill Mob*, was in good financial shape, but was thought to lack the star quality needed to crack foreign markets. The industry's biggest wig, J Arthur Rank, decided to address the problem by imitating the 'star system' used in American studios. They nursed new talent into the public eye by putting young actors through an apprenticeship for stardom, and the Rank Charm School was intended to perform the same function in 50s Britain.

Otherwise known as the 'Company of Youth', Charm School pupils were trained in the techniques of public performance, and were almost all young women. They were expected to behave themselves on or off set, and any kind of scandal, even so much as a mention in gossip columns, was theoretically punishable by suspension of contract. Though the press was always eager to print publicity shots of the girls, most alumni returned to quiet obscurity after a year or two of inert glamour – but the School did give the world Diana Dors, the most convincing Hollywood-style sex symbol of her day, and the indefatigably successful Joan Collins.

Screen Glare

British television still inhabited a quiet cultural backwater, and was treated as a second-class medium by the BBC, but in 1951 it scored its first palpable hit. *What's My Line* was a copy of an American show, and made its British debut in July, soon achieving an astonishing audience of a million people. Its success turned 'panellists' into a respectable way of earning a living, and made the nation's first TV star of presenter Gilbert Harding.

Essentially a current affairs debate, *What's My Line* was supposed to present a balance of brains, beauty and 'personality'. Panels tended to include well-mannered, educated ladies such as Lady Isobel Barnett and Barbara Kelly, but the real attraction was Harding, whose grumpy impatience with fools and fudgers made a huge impression. Harding became a voice of national authority, though he hated the importance with which his every utterance was greeted and disliked being in the public eye. Long after his fame had subsided, in 1959, Harding staggered back into the spotlight by opening his heart to the nation, and weeping, during an interview by one of his successors, Malcolm Muggeridge. He died suddenly a few weeks later, and was publicly mourned in a way he might well have despised.

Yesterday's Men

The last echoes of the Festival of Britain faded on 6 October, when the touring shows finally closed their doors, but the public wasn't about to go quietly back into austerity. Because the King was anxious to see a strong government in office before he left for a tour of New Zealand, October also saw the general election everyone had been anticipating since the last one.

Labour took a majority of the votes cast, but constituency arrangements had their usual decisive say in a close race, and Winston Churchill became prime minister for the second time, with a small but workable majority of 17. For Labour, Attlee remained at the helm, though he was without Cripps and Ernest Bevin, who both died shortly after the election, as well as Bevan, who had resigned in April over the imposition of prescription charges to pay for British forces in Korea. The Liberals could only fight a limited campaign and sank to a new low of six MPs.

The new government wasted no time in having the South Bank site cleared, as if it might prompt happy memories of austerity, but the spirit of a national knees-up lingered on in a craze for 'Festival style'.

Gilbert Harding looks characteristically glum as he listens to an after-dinner speaker. Harding was a troubled man, frequently unimpressed by the quality of life around him, and had become nationally famous for saying so.

Winston Churchill, wife Clementine at his side, acknowledges his constituency victory on election night, already aware that he will be back in Number 10 by morning. At 78, Churchill wasn't expected to tarry long before retiring, but instead tested the affection of party and public by clinging to office until 1955.

Festival Style

Festival Style meant bright colours, often displayed on carpets, walls, or the ends of buildings in wild mosaics or jagged, jazzy patterns. Festival Style, or 'contemporary style', was self-consciously modern and upbeat, featuring steel and aluminium structures of all sizes. Chairs at the Festival, designed by Ernest Race, had been made of moulded steel rods, and Festival Style embraced all sorts of furniture with similar sci-fi echoes, generally made of new, upbeat materials such as plastic, fibre-glass, plywood or Formica.

Festival Style didn't last long, and never really extended into the worlds of high fashion, fine art or music. But it was Britain's first real attempt at cultural self-expression since the War and it sowed seeds that would gradually help British pop culture develop an identity of its own.

OTHER NEWS...

... Seoul falls to Communist forces on 4 January... the first colour televisions reach the US market... JD Salinger's *The Catcher in the Rye*... UN forces recapture Seoul in March... 1 April, first NHS prescription charge: one shilling... Julius and Ethel Rosenberg found guilty... submarine *HMS Affray* sinks off Alderney, metal fatigue blamed... 22 April, Nye Bevan resigns as Health Minister... Newcastle beat Blackpool 2-0 at Wembley, no winner's medal yet for Stanley Matthews... Celtic win the Scots Cup, Hibs the league... Americans and Australians dominate Wimbledon... the British film censor introduces X certificates... no X certificates for Hitchcock's *Strangers On A Train*, Brando in *A Streetcar Named Desire* or Oscar-winner *An American in Paris*... Abdullah, King of Jordan, is assassinated in July... Royal Commission on Marriage and Divorce is established to investigate rising UK divorce rates... Hammer Films sets up a permanent studio at Bray... Isaac Asimov's *Foundation*, and John Wyndham's British blockbuster *The Day of the Triffids*... Florence Chadwick is the first woman to swim the English Channel... Juan Péron is re-elected president of Argentina... South Africans compelled to carry ID Cards identifying them by race... 48 countries recognise Japan's sovereignty... Egypt bans Israel-bound shipping from the Suez Canal, and renounces its treaty with Britain when the UN protests... George VI undergoes lung surgery in September... *Hello Young Lovers*, *Kisses Sweeter than Wine* and *Unforgettable* are all hit songs... Vaughan Williams' opera *The Pilgrim's Progress* premieres at the Royal Festival Hall... 'Sugar Ray' Robinson wins the world middleweight boxing crown... Dennis the Menace gets into print... the UK bank lending rate rises from 2% to 2.5% in November... Egypt declares a state of emergency in December, and recalls its UK ambassador.... General Certificate of Education introduced to schools... goodbye: Fanny Brice, Henri-Philippe Petain, Arnold Schoenberg, Crown Prince Wilhelm of Germany, Ludwig Wittgenstein...

John Huston's *The African Queen* was a huge box office hit, and redefined the career of an ageing Humphrey Bogart. It also made extensive use of British production and technical facilities, helping establish a link with Hollywood that has been keeping home studios in business ever since.

Ties that bind

The Royal Family had been in crisis before the Second World War, shaken by the scandals surrounding Edward VIII's abdication and marriage. The essentially modest George VI had behaved impeccably ever since, and the whole family had won the nation's genuine affection by remaining in London during the worst of the Blitz. The King, whose health had been causing popular concern for some time, fell seriously ill in the latter part of 1951, and died of lung cancer on 6 February.

George's 25-year-old eldest daughter, the much admired Princess Elizabeth, rushed home from a Kenyan tour to assume the throne, but Britons would not truly become 'New Elizabethans' until her spectacular coronation more than a year later. Meanwhile the King's state funeral, on 15 February, might have been a requiem for the world he represented, the one in which Britain pulled the strings.

George VI's coffin is escorted to Paddington, en route for burial in Windsor. The huge crowd, and its genuine grief, bore witness to the King's quietly successful restoration of his family's reputation.

Frontlines

Conscription was in force throughout the 50s, and was never remotely popular, but it was widely accepted that trained troops were needed to police a turbulent world and to defend Britain against possible Soviet attack.

Fear of the USSR bound together western European countries that were already partners in NATO, as never before, and their frontiers with the Iron Curtain were fraught with uncertainties. East Germany closed its borders around partitioned Berlin that summer, but West Berlin still reported about 16,000 escapees from the East in August, while the execution of Czech dissidents by a Stalinist regime reminded everyone why the refugees kept coming. Britain could stand aloof from a network of new continental treaties that were edging France and Germany towards a common market, but its defence commitment, in Europe and at home, could hardly be reduced. At the same time Britain was obliged to address the challenge of nationalism facing its empire, especially in Egypt and, from the autumn, in Kenya. These hotspots took troops, lots of them, and as long as Britain was tangled up in imperial wars, young men would be receiving their call-up papers.

Soapbox

The King's funeral was broadcast on television, as well as radio, but the government was hardly interested in the new box and Churchill himself thought it an irrelevant triviality. So did Dwight D Eisenhower, recently retired as the US Army's commander in Europe, who banished TV cameras when he announced his presidential candidacy.

Ike's sponsors, the Republican Party, felt very differently, and the 1952 campaign became a televised sloganeering contest, with each side spending around $8 million on advertising and 'I Like Ike' emerging as the clear winner.

East Germans, many separated from families by the country's partition, clamour for asylum at a West Berlin reception centre. In the early 50s, before Soviet clampdowns and checkpoints stifled the flow, scenes like this were an everyday sight in Berlin.

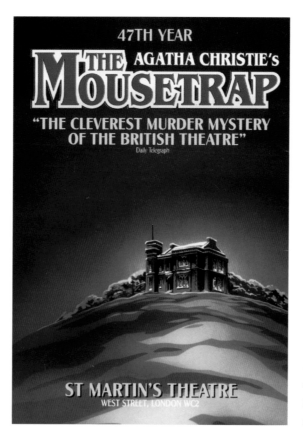

47TH YEAR

AGATHA CHRISTIE's

THE MOUSETRAP

"THE CLEVEREST MURDER MYSTERY OF THE BRITISH THEATRE"
Daily Telegraph

ST MARTIN'S THEATRE
WEST STREET, LONDON WC2

Agatha Christie wrote 66 detective thrillers, and half a dozen novels under the pen-name Mary Westmacott, during a career that spanned more than half a century. She also wrote several plays, one of which, *The Mousetrap*, began a 50-year West End run in 1952.

In 1951, the US Constitution's 22nd Amendment had restricted an individual presidency to two terms, and Truman's place on the Democrat ticket went to Adlai Stevenson, a benign, academic figure in his trade-mark bow tie. With or without advertising's 'motivational psychology', Stevenson's mild good nature stood little chance against a national hero of Eisenhower's stature, and on 4 November Americans voted a Republican into the White House for the first time in more than 20 years.

Hollywood on Trial

Electioneering wasn't television's only contribution to American politics in 1952, because Joe McCarthy's investigations into Communist sympathisers in the movie business were being broadcast to the nation.

Hollywood studio bosses were falling over themselves to cooperate with the Un-American Activities Committee, so that artists, writers and technicians who could not, or would not, clear their names were being consigned to a growing Hollywood blacklist. Some were able to work, but only under pseudonyms and by employing others to impersonate them in public. One such writer, Dalton Trumbo, one of the 'Hollywood Ten' jailed for Communist sympathies in 1951, even won an incognito Oscar for *The Brave One* in 1957, under the pseudonym Robert Rich.

As suspects named other suspects to protect themselves, and McCarthy's net widened, television audiences watched in amazed horror as the Committee's harangues reduced Larry Parks, star of *The Jazz Singer*, to abject distress, and screen tough guy Edward G Robinson gave a craven, apologetic performance, begging for leniency. The Committee's suspicions also fell on British-born Charlie Chaplin, who came to London in October for the premier of *Limelight*. Informed that he would be facing a hearing on his return, Chaplin simply stayed in Europe, where local film industries were benefitting from a steady influx of Hollywood refugees.

The Cruel Sea: great book, great film, great cast, but no first division international stars – a box office handicap that limited the British film industry's international impact throughout the 50s.

Suspects who refused to incriminate anyone other than themselves, like comedian Zero Mostel or folk singing satirist Pete Seeger, were often punished with jail sentences. Playwright Arthur Miller was, however, offered an alternative deal – acquittal if the Committee chairman could pose for a photo with his wife, Marilyn Monroe. Miller refused and was blacklisted, but his plays could still be performed and one, *The Crucible*, would soon expose the Washington 'witch trials' to the ridicule they deserved.

Before the Flood

Musicals were still the great showcase for popular music – this was the year of Gene Kelly's *Singin' In The Rain* – but something new was stirring among American youngsters. They were acquiring a taste for wild dance music with black roots. It was given a name after disc jockey Alan Freed called his new show *Moondog's Rock'n'Roll Party*, and a bad name after a riot broke out at Freed's *Moondog Coronation Ball* in March. Rock'n'roll would finally reach Britain more than two years later, but nothing so childish had infected the music scene by 1952, when the country's first ever pop chart appeared.

On 14 November, the *New Musical Express* published a 'Top Twelve', though dead heats based on very rough calculations meant it listed 15 songs. A snapshot of British musical taste before the 'youthquake' of the later 50s, it was of course dominated by American product. Al Martino's *Here In My Heart* stood at number one, ahead of 78s by Nat 'King' Cole, Rosemary Clooney, Bing Crosby, Frankie Laine, Mario Lanza and Doris Day.

There was nothing very forward looking about the home-grown talent on display. Vera Lynn had no less than three songs in the hit parade and the other local representative was

Green Revolution

In February, the government offered farmers £5 per acre to plough up grassland. The move emphasised an important national priority: ensuring that nothing like the U-Boat campaigns could ever again bring Britain to the brink of starvation. By turning grassland over to crops, with the help of new pesticides, fertilisers and agricultural technology, the government aimed to grow enough food for the nation's needs.

It worked in the short term. New wonder chemicals and hybrid seeds flooded out of corporate laboratories, and Britain has been producing big food surpluses since the 1960s. In the longer term, the 'Green Revolution' created problems that are still being addressed 50 years on. It has been blamed for soil degradation and other environmental problems, while giant, mechanized farms have reduced the variety of food grown, swept aside hedgerows and helped the rapid spread of diseases, decimating the rural labour market in the process.

The same techniques were applied to transform the agriculture of many Third World countries during the 1950s. There have been success stories, especially in Asia, but many African and South American countries have since been plagued by famine, or by economic dependence on high-maintenance export crops.

Max Bygraves. Also there, lurking at number twelve, was the nearest 1952 came to a teen idol – American crooner Johnny Ray, the Nabob of Sob himself, whose act consisted of reducing young women to tears with overblown hymns to heartbreak.

With radio still very much a reflection of adult tastes, the pop charts would be filled with more of the same for the next few years. American stars such as Frank Sinatra, making his first comeback, Dean Martin, Eddie Fisher, Tony Bennett and the Ink Spots all did well, but these were also good times for their native imitators. Singers such as David Whitfield, Dickie Valentine, Ruby Murray and Alma Cogan were big stars in Britain, along with groups such as the Beverly Sisters, the Johnstone Brothers and the Stargazers.

Not all pop music of the early 1950s was inspired by America. The nation's love of light orchestral and big-band sounds gave us Mantiovani, Frank Chacksfield, Billy Cotton, Cyril Stapleton, Ron Goodwin, Ken Mackintosh, Roy Martin, the perennial Ted Heath and many more. Music hall and pub traditions meanwhile made stars of cheerful ivory-tinklers such as Joe 'Mister Piano' Henderson and Winifred Atwell.

Trailblazer

Britain could no longer run the world, or even keep the shops supplied properly, and now it was even losing its place as the great hothouse of inventions and bright ideas.

Britain's adopted piano queen meets the keyboard clown prince of America. Winifred Atwell out-grins a relatively understated Liberace.

1. "It is very cold today," said Bill to Ben.

2. Ben did not answer. "He is frozen stiff," said Bill.

3. Bill shook him and danced him up and down very hard.

4. But Ben stayed as stiff as a board and never said a word.

5. Then Bill fetched some water from the tap in a can.

6. "Perhaps he will melt in this," he said, filling a tub.

7. Suddenly Ben started to laugh. He ran away. Bill was very surprised!

8. "I was only playing," Ben said, "no cold bath for me today, thank you very much!"

Children's superstars Bill and Ben had it tough in the 50s – living rough, sharing a Little Weed, nothing but a comic strip by way of merchandising, and even then they had to hire their own Flobbadobba translator. Life's been easier since they retired in 1970, and these days they're profiting very nicely from videos, T-shirts and gardening consultancy fees.

In 1952 alone, America gave the world polio vaccine, the combine harvester, videotape, the contraceptive pill (still a long way from public use), frozen peas, car seat belts, whitening toothpaste and Buckminster Fuller's geodesic dome home. Meanwhile in Japan, soon to be the world's gadget supplier, Sony was putting the first transistor radios on the market. All very well, but what the British public, newsreels and newspapers wanted were British 'firsts', and when they got one they really went to town.

The first jet airliner, the British De Havilland Comet, opened BOAC services from Heathrow on 2 May, years ahead of rival French, American and Soviet projects. Its first flight took passengers to Johannesburg, and needed to make five stops en route. The press and aviation experts flew into ecstasies, jet travel was suddenly a crucial step forward for humanity, and the planes themselves sold like hot cakes all over the world.

At a time when every European country, especially Britain, was frantically looking for new ways to earn overseas income, the air-travel market looked a good bet for the future. The first non-stop flights from Europe to Japan, across the Arctic Circle, also began in 1952. The last transatlantic blue riband was won by the *SS United States* in three days, ten hours and 40 minutes. The journey took less than 11 hours by passenger jet, a fact that finally doomed the giant ocean liners to extinction and made the Comet seem such a perfect symbol of British resurgence.

Sadly, the Comet story went horribly wrong. Much was made of the aircraft's daringly innovative design, but a year later the planes started exploding in mid-air. Metal fatigue and faulty layout design were blamed, and in 1954 all Comets were grounded. They stayed on the ground for four years, by which time Britain's head start had been lost to the French Caravelle and two superior American jets, the Boeing 707 and the Douglas DC-8.

Power Games

Even the newsreels couldn't manufacture much home glory out of that summer's Olympic Games in Helsinki, where the equestrian team won Britain's solitary gold medal. The star of the show was Czech runner Emil Zatopek, his face locked in a tight grimace as he won the 5,000-metre, 10,000-metre and marathon titles, a feat previously considered impossible. These were the first Games to feature the USSR, and the first dominated by the superpower rivalry that would taint future events. Zatopek's achievements were hailed as a political triumph by

Yes, they are all waving to an airliner, but not just any airliner. This is the De Havilland Comet, the world's first jetliner, about to begin its inaugural scheduled flight from an early incarnation of Heathrow.

Czechoslovakia's Communist regime, and he became a national treasure, but he would fall foul of the same authorities during the 'Prague spring' of 1968.

Honky Tonk Woman

Born in Trinidad, pianist Winifred Atwell was a big star in Britain throughout the 1950s. She came to London, via America, in the late 1940s, and played ragtime piano in jazz clubs to finance her studies at the Royal Academy of Music. By 1951 she had been picked up by the country's top record label, Decca, and went on to have a string of hits, topping the charts in 1954 with *Let's Have Another Party*, and with *Poor People of Paris* in 1956.

The 'Rag Queen' was also an early television stalwart. Regular TV appearances, with an act that mixed classical pieces and her honky-tonk hits, extended her career as audiences expanded, but she never returned to the charts after reaching the Top Ten with *Piano Party* at the end of 1959. Thanks to the BBC, one Winifred Atwell number did enjoy a rather longer shelf life, after her *Black And White Rag* became the signature tune for *Pot Black*.

The Smoke

London was infamous for its fogs, and they had been turning increasingly nasty as the number of coal-burning domestic and industrial fires grew. By the 1950s, people living in London and other major cities were familiar with smog. London smogs – filthy, yellow and opaque – had caused breathing problems and killed people before. They worsened after a cash-strapped government began selling the cleanest British coal abroad, and keeping 'dirty' brown coal for domestic use. Though this was not public knowledge, there had been

A deadly dull morning in Town. London traffic crawls through Blackfriars in the unnatural gloom of December's lethal smog.

calls for something to be done about smogs, but nothing happened until tragedy struck the capital in early December.

For five days, a blanket of cold air was becalmed over London, forcing smoky air from homes and power stations to cool and fall back to the ground. A sulphurous, soot-laden, pea souper settled on the streets, reducing visibility to inches and bringing the city to a halt.

Traffic and trains were paralysed, theatres and cinemas closed because audiences couldn't see the shows, prize cattle expired at the Smithfield Show, and 4000 Londoners died. The majority died of respiratory failure and London's undertakers ran out of coffins.

In the aftermath, air pollution could no longer be dismissed as the price of progress, and the government's inquiry recommended a Clean Air Act, restricting the use of solid fuels in urban areas. The world's first such law, it came into force in 1956. Less virulent smogs still occasionally plagued London and provincial cities in the late 1950s, but smokeless fuels and central heating had eradicated poisonous pea soupers within another decade.

OTHER NEWS...

... US and Britain agree on mutual consent before any nuclear attack on the USSR... the South African Supreme Court declares apartheid illegal, but the government declares parliament a higher court... Winter Olympics open in Oslo... UK identity cards abolished on 21 February... Greece and Turkey join NATO in February... the US begins bombing North Korean power plants... China accuses the US of using germ warfare... nuclear explosion shown live on US network television in April... France and West Germany in dispute over Saar border province... goal-scorer George Robledo helps Newcastle win the Cup again, beating Arsenal at Wembley... Manchester United's first post-War title, and Hibs for the second year running in Scotland... riots and demonstrations hit South African cities in June... Australian Frank Sedgeman wins Wimbledon men's singles, and American Maureen Connelly wins her first ladies' title... the last London tram runs from Woolwich to New Cross on 5 July... the USA heads the Olympic medals table, USSR second... Britain's haul is one gold, two silver and eight bronze medals... Egyptian revolution erupts on 23 July; King Farouk I abdicates in favour of his infant son and flees to Italy... an early UNIVAC computer predicts the US election result before the polls close...Paris Treaty establishes the European Defence Community, an early step towards the Common Market... Dylan Thomas is the first author to record a taped book of his poems... Communists gain control of the countryside in French Vietnam.... Ernest Hemingway releases *The Old Man and the Sea*, Harold Robbins *A Stone for Danny Fisher*, John Steinbeck *East of Eden*, EB White *Charlotte's Web*... *Angels One-Five* is a British cinema hit.... Rocky Marciano takes the world heavyweight crown from Jersey Joe Walcott....Scrabble is launched... Albert Schweitzer wins the Nobel peace prize... French authorities arrest Moroccan nationalists in December... Bill and Ben first shown on TV... goodbye: Agatha Christie, Eva Peron, Chaim Weizmann

Eyes forward

Despite all the positive spin of the previous few years, it was not until 1953 that the country shed its post-War hand-me-downs and got properly dressed up for an adventurous future. All sorts of social and economic factors helped get Britain into its glad rags, but one big day stood out for all the world to see – the fantastically successful coronation of Queen Elizabeth the Second.

The Big Parade

Apart from a very British spell of wet weather, everything about the Coronation seemed to go perfectly, even the omens surrounding it. In February, Cambridge chemists Francis Crick and James Watson, with help from Maurice Wilkins and Rosalind Franklin, had described the double helix structure of human DNA. Destined to be of enormous worldwide significance, their work was a boost to the country's recovering ego. Churchill too did his characteristic bit for national prestige, accepting a hero's welcome on his visit to meet the new American president, an old wartime colleague, and ending the year with the Nobel literature prize for his *History of the English Speaking Peoples*.

The Queen, wearing her new crown, is joined by Charles, Anne and Philip as she greets crowds from the balcony of Buckingham Palace.

THE ONLY FULL LENGTH TECHNICOLOR FILM OF THE CORONATION

A QUEEN IS CROWNED .ᵤ

Colour by TECHNICOLOR

THE SCENES INCLUDE THE CROWNING
CEREMONY IN WESTMINSTER ABBEY

Produced by   Narration by   Written by   Musical Adviser   Special music by
CASTLETON KNIGHT   SIR LAURENCE OLIVIER   CHRISTOPHER FRY   SIR MALCOLM SARGENT   GUY WARRACK   THE LONDON SYMPHONY ORCHES

Colour television was already widely available in America, but still more than a decade away in Britain, so Technicolor was the key to this movie's enormous success in the home market.

On May 29, with house parties, street parties and civic events being prepared all over the country, word came from the Himalayas that climber Edmund Hillary and his Sherpa guide Tensing Norgay had become the first to conquer Mount Everest. Hillary was a New Zealander, but he was a subject of the Queen so his triumph was instantly adopted by the nation as a perfect Coronation gift.

The Coronation itself took place in Westminster Abbey on 2 June. A vast canvas of colour, crowds and solemn pageant, graced by the world's dignitaries, it centred on a lovely young Queen who seemed to have not an enemy in the world as she was cheered to and from the Abbey by vast crowds of well-wishers. The multitudes jamming London's streets could not, of course, see the ceremony itself, but some 20 million people could, on three million TV sets in homes and halls throughout the land. What they saw finally made up their minds about television.

Royal Box

The BBC nearly didn't get to show the Coronation at all. The Palace committee, headed by the Archbishop of Canterbury and the Duke of Norfolk, refused the first request, and only changed its mind after months of persuasion that television wouldn't intrude on the ceremony. To make sure, capacious commentator Richard Dimbleby was required to address the watching nation from a tiny, uncomfortable hideaway in the Abbey roof. He still gave a brilliant performance that caught the mood of pride, gravitas and celebration to a tee, and set the standard for television's tone in the presence of history.

American viewers could get colour TV by 1953, and the number one US show – *I Love Lucy* – pulled in a staggering 50 million audience when Lucille Ball's character and the actress herself gave birth on the same day. In Britain it was still rare to have 'the television' – a tall cabinet in mahogany or teak, with doors protecting the modesty of its tiny screen – and the programmes on offer were generally a lot less exciting.

At the start of the decade, the BBC took a worthy approach to programming, offering cooking classes with Philip Narben, gardening with Fred Streeter or Eric Robinson's *Music For You*; along with second-rate light entertainment and earnest panel games. Children fared a little better, and seemed to genuinely enjoy the antics of Andy Pandy, Bill and Ben or

Len Hutton, the first professional to captain England at cricket, leads his team out for the 1953 Oval test against Australia. On his right, Surrey spinner Alec Bedser, who had demolished the Australians with 19 wickets at the Old Trafford test.

350-MILE HAVOC

This is one of the terror towns

Hundreds dead and missing in biggest sea flood disaster

DAILY SKETCH 2d

AND DAILY GRAPHIC

CANVEY ISLAND, 150 FEARED DEAD

STORY BEGINS ON PAGE 2
PAGES OF PICTURES INSIDE

Gatecrasher

A year of triumph had begun with tragedy. With the shock of December's smog still fresh in the memory, a more truly natural disaster hit the east coast of England on the last evening of January. The freak combination of a strong storm surge and an unusually high tide brought a sudden rise of up to six feet in local sea levels, and caused havoc from the Thames to the Humber.

More than 30,000 people were evacuated from flooded areas, some 24,000 homes were damaged or destroyed and 307 people lost their lives. Sixty-six were killed at Heacham, in Norfolk, and 58 on Canvey Island, which virtually disappeared under water. London, where water was lapping at the tops of the Chelsea and Victoria embankments, barely escaped a second catastrophe.

Muffin The Mule. Children's programmes began at three in the afternoon, or at five on Sundays, and the BBC closed down for an hour at six so that youngsters could be put to bed. All broadcasting ended at half past ten, but the BBC struggled to fill even that much space, so viewers were treated to frequent interludes of 'soothing' images and music.

British TV slowly grew a little more ambitious. The first broadcast between countries was shown in a 1952 Paris Panorama, hosted by Richard Dimbleby and Sylvia Peters, and the budget speech was televised in April 1953. A raft of ground-breaking programmes, including *The Quatermass Experiment*, were ready for broadcast later in the year, but it still took a pre-Coronation surge to bring the number of household sets above three million in time for the event.

Television ownership increased more rapidly afterwards, but Britain's film industry still didn't have much to worry about. With audiences still essentially captive, British films such as *The Cruel Sea* were matching more lavish American product at the box office, and almost anything shown in the cinema could turn a profit. When Rank's *A Queen is Crowned* became a box-office smash, one trade paper felt able to dismiss the BBC broadcast as 'the finest and most widely distributed trailer in the annals of show business.'

S-e-x

In the early 1950s, as a generation raised before the War took on adulthood and marriage, young people seemed bent on recreating the lives of their parents. Surveys taken in 1950 showed that not only the vast majority of young women, but also more than half of the young men questioned, thought sex outside marriage was wrong. Austerity and prurience seemed to go together, but orthodox attitudes towards sex took a real battering in 1953.

In America, Hugh Hefner launched the first issue of *Playboy* magazine, and made a fine profit in spite of prosecution for sending pornography through the US Mail. Hollywood meanwhile gave the Oscar for best picture to *From Here To Eternity*, complete with notorious surf-bound love scenes, while nobody was pretending Jane Russell and Marilyn Monroe were anything but sex symbols in *Gentlemen Prefer Blondes*. The French, inevitably, got in on the act. The Cannes Film Festival couldn't get enough of teenage 'nymphet' Brigitte Bardot, tousled, pouting and barely dressed in a scruffy sweater. Even the British hit film *Genevieve* caused a mild stir by hinting at a 'dirty' weekend in Brighton, but that was nothing compared to the behaviour of James Bond, who arrived in 1953, boozing and bedding his way through Ian Fleming's *Casino Royale*.

An American sociologist, Alfred C. Kinsey, added an academic voice to the mix with his report, *Sexual Behavior in the American Female*, which upset all sorts of upright citizens and churchmen by claiming that women, by and large, enjoyed sex. Meanwhile, English publication of *The Second Sex* by Simone de Beauvoir made a catchphrase of the term 'women's liberation'. The age of popular 'voyeur sex' was beginning, but the age of straightforward gender roles was coming to an end.

Muddied But Unbowed

Even the cosy world of British sport felt the jolt of a fresh breeze in 1953. There were marvellous, old-fashioned moments, but they were framed by the shock of the new. England's cricketers won a captivating Ashes series, but the real story at Lord's was the appointment as captain of Yorkshire's Len Hutton, a professional rather than a gentleman amateur. Meanwhile, at Wembley, an amazing and heart-warming cup final was offset by the unforgettable demolition of England's football pride.

When Blackpool beat Bolton 4-3 to win the Cup, after a thrilling finish, veteran England winger Stanley Matthews earned a winner's medal at the third attempt. One of football's best-loved heroes, the 'wizard of the dribble' had played brilliantly in what was assumed to be his swansong. In fact Matthews was still playing top flight football more than a decade later, and finally retired at 53.

The rosy glow of May was gone in late November, when England played Hungary in a friendly. England had never lost at Wembley to a team from outside the British Isles, a proud record that sustained British football's faith in its own superiority. A magnificent Hungarian team, led by 'Galloping Major' Ferenc Puskas, played a strong England side off the park, and was unlucky to only win 6-3. Some people still said it was a one-off, but not after the rematch in Budapest ended as a 7-1 humiliation. Hungary went on to grace, but not win, the 1954 World Cup, while English football licked its wounds, slowly shed the myth of its invincibility, and began a rethink that would eventually bear fruit in 1966.

Watched by Stanley Rous and a starstruck Duke of Edinburgh, the new queen presents Stanley Matthews with his 1953 cup winner's medal.

THE BIG CHANGE IN TV

(L.) *Headliner 21* (21T6082). Ebony finish, $199.95 Stand, optional, extra. (R) *Gladstone 21* (21T635). Mahogany grained finish, $269.95. Shown, limed oak grained finish, $279.95.

RCA Victor presents TV's _first_ complete re-styling

No obvious dials or gadgets. Nothing in view but TV's finest picture and most luxurious cabinets!

Here is TV that goes far beyond what you've come to expect. *This* TV is more than mere equipment. It breathes style in every line!

Just imagine how you could transform your living room with one of these smart sets. Take the *Headliner 21*. No controls in sight. What a picture it makes—and what a picture you get! Or, for fine performance and a look of richness that belies its price tag, choose the *Gladstone 21* with "High-Side" tuning. Both sets bring you "4-Plus" picture quality—greater brightness, contrast, steadiness.

Great New TV Advances. For as little as $149.95, new RCA Victor TV brings you the fabulous new "Un-Mechanical Look," TV's first complete re-styling . . . plus new Balanced Fidelity Sound . . .

plus "High-and-Easy" tuning that lets you dial standing up. *And prices are down as much as 18%.*

More models, more unusual finishes, more beauty, more sheer *value* in TV than ever before —exactly what you want—ready for you now at your RCA Victor dealer's.

RCA Factory Service, assuring expert installation and maintenance, is available in most areas—but only to RCA Victor TV owners. Optional, extra.

Manufacturer's nationally advertised VHF list prices shown, subject to change. Slightly higher in far West and South. UHF optional at RCA Victor's lowest price ever—only $25 extra.

See Milton Berle, Martha Raye on NBC-TV alternately, 2 out of every 3 Tuesdays. And don't miss NBC-TV's spectacular "Producers' Showcase" in RCA Compatible Color or black-and-white, Dec. 12.

RCA VICTOR
RADIO CORPORATION OF AMERICA

EVERY YEAR MORE PEOPLE BUY RCA VICTOR THAN ANY OTHER TELEVISION

"4-Plus" Picture Quality. Greater brightness, contrast, steadiness. In sets priced as low as $200.

"Hidden Panel" Tuning. Lets you dial easily—standing up.

By 1953, American television didn't need the Coronation to make it popular, and it didn't have to sneak into living rooms disguised as a cocktail cabinet.

44

Hawk's Eye View

New Elizabethan optimism wasn't having much impact on imperial troubles heating up in Egypt and in Kenya, where Jomo Kenyatta's Mau Mau rebellion gathered force all year. It made no difference at all to the Cold War, which was a shame because 'hawks' were gaining the upper hand in America. McCarthy was at the height of his power, Vice President Richard Nixon had made his name preaching against the Red Menace, and the amiable, golf-obsessed Eisenhower had chosen a real spinechiller as his secretary of state.

John Foster Dulles would come to be seen as America's ultimate Cold Warrior, and would be at the helm of Eisenhower's foreign policy until 1959. He talked a frighteningly tough battle from the start, and he meant it. In 1953, convinced that the USSR was neither strong nor determined enough to risk nuclear war against the West, he announced his intention to confront Communism with 'massive' deterrent force. Dulles, whose brother Alan became head of the CIA in 1953, went on to spend a staggering $350 billion on defence in the next eight years. He backed the investment with unblinking poker player's tactics towards Communist states and anyone helping them, a method he would later describe as 'brinkmanship'.

There was good news out there. The Korean War finally spluttered to an end in July, without plunging everyone into nuclear confrontation. It had still cost UN forces 300,000 dead, killed about three million Koreans and Chinese, and ended as a draw, with the frontier back where it had started. The new Yugoslav president, Marshal Tito, visited London to demonstrate that not all Communist leaders were puppets of Moscow, and Stalin died in March, offering hope of a change in Soviet

'The only case I know of a bull who carries his own china shop.' (Winston Churchill). John Foster Dulles arrives at Heathrow, and gives it the hard stare.

attitudes. A different side to American politics also held the spotlight for a moment in September, when young John Fitzgerald Kennedy married Jacqueline Lee Bouvier, an event shown on newsreels all over the world.

Art Liberated

British sculpture enjoyed worldwide critical acclaim in the 1950s. Barbara Hepworth, Henry Moore and the other great abstract artists of the day were well known to the public, and their works treated with slightly bewildered respect, but more radical, industrial works by artists such as Lynn Chadwick, Kenneth Armitage

As they leave the church in Newport, Rhode Island, Jack Kennedy and his beautiful young bride, Jackie Bouvier, are the golden couple of American politics. A handsome, youthful contrast to Vice-President Nixon and Eisenhower's other likely successors, with an excellent war record to boot, JFK is already being touted as presidential material.

or Reg Butler left many completely mystified. Butler's abstract, The Unknown Political Prisoner, won a cash prize in 1953, prompting howls of derision from the popular press, which could hardly contain its glee when an embittered fellow competitor destroyed the work with an axe.

New Elizabethans

After the show, the rest of the summer was all about adoration of Elizabeth. Crowds and the world's press swarmed to Epsom for Derby Day, soon after the Coronation, almost expecting a royal win to suit the mood, but no-one complained about a first Derby win for the king of jockeys, Gordon Richards. The Queen and Duke Philip then set off on a triumphantly successful tour of New Zealand, setting the tone for years of tireless public relations work all around the Commonwealth, while British people settled down to living in the 'New Elizabethan' age. They wouldn't have to wait long to feel its benefits, because the government had chimed nicely with the general mood by authorising an end to all rationing for 1954.

OTHER NEWS...

... Tito elected president of Yugoslavia... death sentence imposed for taking the Mau Mau oath in Kenya... sweets rationing ends on 4 February... Britain and Egypt agree independence for Sudan in 1956... death of Josef Stalin announced on 6 March... Queen Mary, the widow of George V, dies on 24 March... there are an estimated 27,000 millionaires in the US... Swede Dag Hammarskjøld becomes UN Secretary-General on 31 March... Winston Churchill is knighted on 24 April... the Commons votes to privatise the road haulage industry... Ray Bradbury's *Fahrenheit 451*, John Wyndham's *The Kraken Wakes*... Rangers do the double in Scotland, the English title goes to Highbury... James Baldwin's *Go Tell It On the Mountain* and Ralph Ellison's *Invisible Man* are powerful indictments of racism... South African writer Alan Paton's Liberal Party opposes the new Apartheid system... iron and steel rationing end on 5 May... 19 June, Ethel and Julius Rosenberg executed for treason... East German protesters crushed by the Red Army in June... an American bomber crashes at RAF Heyford... privatisation of the iron and steel industries begins in August... French general strike in August... American reports suggest that smoking causes lung cancer... Senator McCarthy sends two aides to investigate the Voice of America radio network in Europe, where they are ridiculed by the press... sugar rationing ends in September... the British Museum publishes a report proving that the Piltdown Man is a hoax... a brutal and apparently motiveless murder in Provence, where the British Drummond family is butchered by a local farmer... George Marshal wins the Nobel Peace Prize for his post-War aid plan... *Waiting for Godot* by Samuel Beckett opens to bemused approval in Paris... *The Crucible* by Arthur Miller... *The Robe*, starring Richard Burton, is the first CinemaScope movie, and a big hit... *The Cruel Sea* and *Albert RN* set the tone for British competition... Britain condemns Israel for Palestinian massacre... Lavrenti Beria, Soviet deputy premier, is executed... goodbye: Hilaire Belloc, Nigel Bruce, Raoul Dufy, Sergei Prokofiev, Hank Williams...

Worlds in waiting

In the years since the War, the world had been divided into three. Britain and some of its 'white' dominions were among the few relatively rich, 'developed' democracies of the First World, while the Second World consisted of the Soviet-led Communist countries. The rest of the planet, with the somewhat indefinable exception of China, was described as 'developing' and called the Third World.

Some of the Third World, including most of Latin America, had been dependent on US economic dictates since the last century. Most Third-World countries had been controlled by European empires, and a stupendously large part had been ruled by the British. In the early 50s, Britain's sprawling network of colonies and bases had started to creak under nationalist pressure, which threatened to damage the home economy, let in Communism, or both. By 1954 it was easy to feel that the Empire was more of a burden than a blessing.

World Service

National service, in force from 1949 until 1960, brought the burdens of empire into homes all around the country, as young conscripts were asked to perform guard duties over increasingly turbulent imperial outposts. Nationalist troubles had called for police actions in British Guiana, where troops had landed immediately after the Coronation, and Nigeria, which became a federation in 1954. In April, anti-British disturbances broke out in Cyprus, and by that time a long battle for control was flaring up again in Kenya.

The anti-British Mau Mau movement grew stronger in Kenya throughout the 1950s, but mushroomed after colonial authorities

Primary school children get down to some 'Duck and Cover' air-raid drill. The belief that this would protect them from nuclear attack – perfectly reasonable among the under-elevens – wasn't playing so well with grown-ups by the mid-50s.

Cairo, October 1954. Egyptian leader Gamal Nasser and British junior minister Anthony Nutting sign the Anglo-Egyptian Accord. The agreement set terms for a British withdrawal from Suez, but its guarantee that Britain would receive a share of future Canal revenues was destined to be its downfall.

imprisoned nationalist leader Jomo Kenyatta in 1951. Attacks on whites or their 'collaborators' forced the British to declare a state of emergency in October 1952, but trouble worsened again in 1954 and emergency powers remained in force until 1960. During that time, thousands died in inter-tribal conflicts – and about 13,000 Kenyans were killed by the British – but only 32 European fatalities were recorded. Kenyatta was eventually released in 1961, and led Kenya to independence in 1963 as leader of the KANU Party.

Egypt wasn't part of the Empire at all, but Britain had effectively run the country for 70 years as a way of maintaining control over the Suez Canal, which was guarded by some 80,000 British troops. This and other affronts to emerging Egyptian nationalism prompted anti-British riots and a military coup in 1952. The new government eventually settled for the Canal's gradual transfer to partial Egyptian control, but the country seemed about to go critical again when Colonel Gamal Nasser seized power in the spring of 1954. Nasser demanded, and got, an agreement from Britain to a full withdrawal by the middle of 1956, but it was a deal that would come back to haunt its architect, foreign secretary Anthony Eden.

France was having even more trouble with its colonies. By November, when a bitter, eight-year war of independence erupted in Algeria, French forces were being transferred to North Africa from Vietnam, where Paris had been forced to give up altogether. Communist North Vietnamese rebels had driven France out of Indochina with a decisive military victory at Dien Bien Phu in May, and the peace signed in Geneva that July recognised North and South Vietnam as separate states. Dulles and the South Vietnamese weren't having that for a moment. The US refused to recognise the peace and, as it prepared to roll back another Communist frontline with swarms of military 'advisors', people were talking of a new Korea.

It looks like just another submarine, but the new, nuclear-powered USS Nautilus triggered a transformation of the Cold War. Now able to stay at sea almost indefinitely, submarines would soon be able to fire nuclear missiles, consigning to oblivion the idea that a powerful 'first strike' could wipe out all means of retaliation.

BUTLIN'S HOLIDAY CAMP
IT'S QUICKER BY RAIL

Reality may not quite have lived up to the poster's burnished, carnival atmosphere, but a nation emerging from austerity was hungry for seaside holidays, and camps such as this provided all the basic ingredients at an affordable price.

Big Bang Theories

The United States accounted for about six percent of the world's population in 1954, but its citizens owned 60 percent of the world's cars, 58 percent of the telephones and 40 percent of the radios. For now, they also owned 100 percent of the world's hydrogen bombs. On 1 March, America tested an improved one on Bikini Atoll in the Marshall Islands.

The bomb, cheerfully codenamed Bravo, worked rather better than expected, exploding with about a thousand times the force unleashed on Hiroshima, and laying waste to three islands. It was, as one triumphant Congressman put it, a 'bigger bang for your buck', though this was scant consolation to some 200 displaced Bikinians, or to dozens of people caught in the fall-out on neighbouring atolls. It would be decades before their suffering came home to roost, but a more immediate sideshow to the event soon gave chilling force to disgraced physicist Robert Oppenheimer's argument that our weapons were already too big.

A Japanese fishing boat, the *Lucky Dragon*, was 85 miles off Bikini when the H-bomb went up. Crew and catch arrived back in Japan saturated with radiation, and the Japanese stopped eating fish overnight. Six months later, the *Lucky Dragon's* radio operator became the first fatality attributed to radiation poisoning. Suddenly, in Britain and elsewhere, the public became better informed about the hazards and likelihood of radiation exposure. Strontium 90's links with leukaemia became well-known, and fears circulated in 1955 that nuclear tests had turned the rain radioactive. On the other side of the fence, nuclear-powered governments took the line that there was nothing much to worry about, and carried on with development.

Seaside Shuffle

The world may have split into three but for many in the age before cheap air travel, it was still divided into two – home and abroad. Cross-channel ferries were available and, as personal prosperity increased in southern England, day trips to Calais, Boulogne or Dieppe became popular, but most people preferred not to travel abroad, and the vast majority of holidays were taken in Britain.

The mid-50s, when workers' holidays usually lasted no more than two weeks at a fixed time each summer, were a golden age for Britain's seaside towns, especially the great vacation metropolis of Blackpool. Few holidaymakers could afford a family holiday in a hotel, but there were cheaper alternatives. Guest houses were the norm, but camping was popular and the period saw a surge in sales of caravans, which allowed a growing number of car owners to stay by the sea without guest-house

Brando in *The Wild One*: OK, so the hat didn't catch on, but the clothes, the bike and attitude were genuine trendsetters.

costs, rules and regulations. This was also a boom time for holiday camps, which were well established before the War but had now developed the distinctive, unrelentingly cheery, character that kept the crowds rolling into Warners, Pontins and Butlins all through the decade.

Thanks For Nothing

Jackson Pollock and Picasso may have been in the vanguard of modern action and abstract painting, and they were much admired here, but in 1954 Graham Sutherland's portrait of Churchill was the most famous painting in Britain, not least because of persistent (and accurate) rumours that the great man himself detested it. Presented to Churchill after he announced his imminent retirement from the Commons, it then disappeared from sight, and his wife later admitted to having the portrait destroyed.

Wild Childish

Popular fashion has never quite recovered from the sight of Marlon Brando's tee shirt and jeans in *The Wild One*. It was a good year for Brando, who also won an Oscar for his performance in *On The Waterfront*, and was undoubtedly Hollywood's hottest star. He was also something new in pop culture – a rebel. Living his volatile and surly screen image

Fair Game

By 1954, the official world mile record had dropped to 4 minutes 1.4 seconds, held jointly by two Swedes, and it was only a matter of time before someone ran the distance in less than four minutes. Roger Bannister, a 25 year-old medical student in his final year, was one of several athletes who looked ready to break the magic barrier.

Though eagerly anticipated, his race on 6 May was a spit and sawdust affair compared with modern sporting extravaganzas. It was held at Oxford's modest Iffley Road track, where Bannister was running for the Amateur Athletic Association in its annual match with the University. Future politician and fellow international Christopher Chataway acted as pacemaker, leading Bannister through the vital third lap to reach the three-quarter mile mark in a whisker above three minutes. Bannister took over with about 350 yards to go, surged to break the tape in 3 minutes, 59.4 seconds, and collapsed into the arms of his trainers.

to the hilt, Brando made a business of outraging Hollywood decencies whenever possible and was duly adored by the young. His dress and manners formed part of an emerging set of images that would soon stand for youth rebellion on both sides of the Atlantic.

Paper Tiger

Joe McCarthy's hold over the American people snapped in 1954, when he overplayed his hand on television and a senior military attorney called his bluff. When US Army lawyer Joseph Welch looked McCarthy in the eye and asked him a straight question – 'Have you left no sense of decency?' – it was as if a spell had been broken. McCarthy was suddenly subjected to ridicule in the press, and was finally toppled after a damning documentary by American TV's voice of conscience, Ed Murrow. At the end of the year, McCarthy received a Senate censure for his behaviour, and remained a powerless fringe figure until heavy drinking killed him in 1957. Fear of the Red Menace would flourish for a few more years without him.

Milk and Alcohol

The drink had killed 39 year-old Dylan Thomas in November 1953, not long after he had finally completed *Under Milk Wood*. The work had been commissioned by BBC radio, and after making his friends there wait for years Thomas had lost the manuscript before boarding a boat to his death in New York. BBC producer Douglas Clevedon eventually found *Under Milk Wood*, tidied it up and broadcast it for the first time in 1954, with Richard Burton as narrator. Its success helped establish the Third Programme's reputation as the BBC's most interesting service.

Faith Spieler

The most famous clergyman of the age was not the Pope, but crusading, born again trader Billy Graham. A former brush salesman, who unashamedly used hard sell techinques to promote his Baptist faith, Graham was at the peak of a career that would prosper into the 1980s. He not only played to packed houses wherever he appeared – two million saw him during a 1954 tour of Britain, his first overseas 'crusade' – but at some time or other during the decade exchanged ideas with most of the world's spiritual and political leaders.

Billy Graham – the man who unleashed religion-as-theatre on the consumer world – socks it to them at London's Harringay Arena. Graham's 1954 British tour, his first outside America, was a triumphant sell-out, establishing him as an international star of stage and steam.

Half-term Report

The 50s were half way through, and it had been a full decade since the War. How was Britain doing?

In some ways, the country was clearly on the up. Rationing had ended in July, the shops had filled up and the welfare state was running in something like its promised form. The country was politically stable, with full employment and a young monarch still enjoying extraordinary popularity. Manufacturing industries, particularly the car firms that seemed so important to Britain's future, were slowly recovering their export potential, while our scientists, artists and thinkers still enjoyed worldwide eminence.

On the other hand, the Empire was disintegrating, and the world at large had become a stand off between two superpowers, with Britain among the also-rans. In many fields, especially economic growth and national wealth, Britain was being overtaken by more than just the superpowers. There were reasons to envy France and Italy their lifestyles, West Germany and Japan their growing economic confidence, and Australia its limitless space and resources.

All in all, life in 1954 offered plenty of nourishment for the green shoots of youthful impatience, and not quite enough affluence for them to get a wider hearing, but there were signs across the Atlantic that the balance would soon be changing.

In America, just as in 1950, the future was already happening. By now, more than half of all American homes had TV, while MacDonald's and Kentucky Fried Chicken were about to join Burger King in a booming fast-food market. A record called *Shboom* had already brought the unmistakable sound of rock 'n' roll to the US pop charts for the first time, and down in Memphis, Tennessee, a kid called Elvis had just cut his first two songs for local label boss Sam Philips.

OTHER NEWS...

... on 2 January, the Pope calls television a threat to family life; in June, he opens the new Eurovision service... the first weatherman appears on British television... ...14 January, Marilyn Monroe marries US baseball player Joe DiMaggio... Billie Holiday begins her first European tour... work begins on the GPO Tower, but it won't open until 1965... SEATO, modelled on NATO, is formed by the US, the UK and six southeast Asian nations.... *On the Waterfront* wins best picture Oscar... also at the movies: *The Caine Mutiny*, *The Day the Earth Stood Still*, *Rear Window*, *20,000 Leagues Under the Sea*, *Bad Day at Black Rock*, *A Star Is Born*... Malenkov becomes premier in the USSR.... the first British TV soap, *The Grove Family*, is shown in April... at Wembley, West Bromwich Albion 3, Preston 2... the US Supreme Court rules against segregation in public schools in May... Robert Oppenheimer loses American security clearance in June... the USSR opens its first nuclear power station.... Mo Connelly makes it a hat trick at Wimbledon... Ken Rosewall loses his first men's final to Jaroslav Drobny, an Egyptian exile from Communist Czechoslovakia, who later became a British Citizen ... 3 July, meat is the last item to come off rationing... Britain sponsors an expedition to search for the Abominable Snowman... Ed Murrow's current affairs show, *See It Now*, wins 20 US TV awards, but will lose its prime time slot to *Beat The Clock* in 1955... Eurovision televises live world cup football from Switzerland... West Germany wins the tournament, beating Hungary in the final... Scotland out in the first round, England in the second... after intense national debate, the British Television Bill becomes law at the end of July, authorising a commercial TV channel... *Lord of the Flies* by William Golding, *Live and Let Die* by Ian Fleming, JRR Tolkein's *The Fellowship of the Ring*... America invents the solar cell... October 20, four-week UK dock strike begins... the Dow Jones industrial index reaches 381, overtaking its pre-Crash high... goodbye: Lionel Barrymore, Colette, Henri Matisse, Alan Turing...

A **generation of children** who didn't remember life before the War had become teenagers, and an expanding education system was offering them a better shot at life's glittering prizes. The products of grammar schools, 'redbrick' universities and new campus-based or 'technical' universities were already bringing an everyman edge to the arts – but in 1955 the vast majority of pupils still left school at the first opportunity.

Most would find jobs without too much trouble, and economic growth – announced from the Devil's own pulpit, advertising – would provide interesting new ways for them to spend their wages. Young women were often still dependent on their families, but boys between 16 and 21 were becoming consumers in the modern sense.

Their parents were becoming more prosperous too, but were often appalled by what their sons wanted to do with all that money. Just a few years earlier, teenagers had been politely aping their elders. Suddenly, they seemed to be modelling themselves on sociopaths and over-excited zoo animals.

Good, Clean Fun

The first rumblings of what came to be called a 'youthquake' in the late 50s passed a lot of

Someone, somewhere probably owned a kitchen like this in the mid-50s, but only if they were very rich or living in America. For most British housewives, its designer touches, built-in cookers, breakfast bar, telephone, non-stick saucepans and mountains of food would be the stuff of fantasy for another 20 years or so.

James Dean, a few months before his death, on the set of *Rebel Without A Cause*. He could be as mean looking and rebellious as Brando, his great rival as a teen heartthrob, but it was the vulnerability that gave Jimmy Dean his extra romantic edge.

people by, and were sometimes quite hard to find. Even among the young, 1955 wasn't a bad year for traditional values.

The Duke of Edinburgh's award scheme began encouraging social conscience in older children, and old-fashioned fun got its own shrine when Disneyland opened in California. A few miles down the road, Disney also gave Hollywood its biggest hit of the decade, and there was nothing very rebellious about *The Lady And The Tramp*.

But the signs were there. A bumper crop of science-fiction movies, including *This Island Earth, 20,000 Leagues Under The Sea* and two British *Quatermass* films, were aimed squarely at the teen market, and one tragic youth idol, James Dean, was the biggest thing in Hollywood that year.

The pop charts were dominated by the usual safe, adult melodies – until the late autumn, when the youth craze that had swept America engulfed Britain. It came in the form of a run-of-the-mill movie – Sterling Hayden in *The Blackboard Jungle* – preceded by a wildly popular title song, *Rock Around the Clock*. Teenage dancing, and whether or not it was antisocial, was suddenly a national issue for the first time, but not for the last.

Fast and... Fidgety

James Dean hit the big time in 1955 with *East of Eden*. His restless, edgy performance, coupled with vulnerable good looks and plenty of introspection, catapulted him to stardom as a teen heart-throb, bigger even than Marlon Brando. Off screen, the two stars seemed to be competing for the title of Hollywood's wildest young rebel, but not for long. At the end of September, at 24, Dean guaranteed himself a place in teenage folklore by dying in a high speed car smash, soon after recording a particularly surly road safety slot for television. His second film, *Rebel Without A Cause*, was released shortly afterwards, and made him a bigger star dead than he had been alive. He was given the first posthumous Oscar for best actor, and Hollywood mourned the loss of a shining light.

One, Two, Three O'Clock...

Britain had heard some rock'n'roll before, and rotund, 30ish Bill Haley wasn't new to the British charts. His latest single, *Rock Around The Clock*, had made only a fleeting chart appearance in January, but that was before it got genuine mass exposure at everyone's local Odeon or Gaumont.

Word of riotous scenes at American cinemas had crossed the Atlantic, but only a few local authorities chose not to allow screenings of *The Blackboard Jungle*, and the rest of the country's youth went wild for what was, in effect, a three-minute concert. A few seats were ripped up during a lot of unlicensed dancing, but there were no riots, though violence was reported in south and east London, where early Teddy Boys were earning a bad reputation for thuggery.

Rock Around The Clock hit the top 20 for the first time in late November and was number one for two spells separated by Christmas. By the time Ernie Ford's *Sixteen Tons* took over in late January, rock'n'roll was firmly in place as the teenage craze of the moment. Whether it was here to stay remained to be seen.

Young Edwardians

The big, greased quiff, like a wave breaking... the sideburns... the long 'drape' jacket, with velvet collar and cuffs.. 'slim Jim' tie... drain-pipe trousers over bright ankle socks... you couldn't miss a Teddy Boy. Modelled on Edwardian gangs of thieving 'cosh boys', Teds began life as something very similar in early 50s south London. The term first appeared in the press late in 1953, when Elvis was still a truck driver, but Teddy Boys were more notorious than numerous until rock'n'roll came along. Suddenly the look, especially the hair, was as fashionable as it was distinctively youthful. For the rest of the decade, there were two kinds of Teddy Boy – thuggish petty criminals, little different from street gangs all over the urban world, and young men making a style statement, most of whom tended to hang up their drape jackets after a spell of national service.

Work all week, dress up a bit, show off the quiff and dance.

Sex Queenie

Rank starlet Diana Dors made herself famous at the 1955 Venice Film Festival by appearing, paddling a gondola, in a rhinestone-encrusted mink bikini. The buxom 23 year-old went on to moderate success as a home-grown version of the Hollywood sex symbol. She couldn't really sing, she didn't become much of an actress until later in her career, and her 'glamour' was always more rhinestone than diamond, but Diana Dors had been well trained at the Charm School, and she was a lot more accessible to the British press than Marilyn Monroe.

For The Responsible Customer

Teenagers weren't alone in enjoying increased purchasing power by 1955. Though few young families yet owned their own homes, the year saw a surge in sales of household goods such as televisions, refrigerators and washing machines, not least because they were getting cheaper and easier to come by. The new Hotpoint twin-tub, for instance, was down to a relatively affordable 75 guineas (£78.75), and minor kitchen luxuries such as food mixers, electric kettles and toasters were becoming more common. Newly invented non-stick saucepans were still a fantasy for most, but everybody could now get aluminium pans to replace all those melted down for war use, while the latest wipe-down surfaces added gleam to the kitchen dream.

This was the image – peroxide blonde, mink bikini, high heels – that made a star of Diana Dors, the most successful of many attempts by British film studios to copy Hollywood's version of sex appeal.

The 'contemporary' home of the mid-50s, still displaying traces of Festival Style, may look a touch gaudy and spindly to modern eyes, but it was a definite change from dowdy pre-War restraint.

Once the same young couples became parents, new ideas about how to raise children were flooding across the Atlantic. None were more influential than those of Dr Benjamin Spock, whose *Baby and Child Care* finally reached Britain in 1955. Spock's stress on the importance of loving common sense – 'You know more than you think you do' – made him a guru of self-help and self-confidence, and the book eventually sold some 20 million copies all over the world.

Civilisation Ends!

After a lot of public agonising, the Television Act had been passed in 1954, authorising the creation of ITV. Right up until the evening the new service began – on 22 September, 1955 – prophets of doom were issuing dire warnings about the effects of 'sponsored broadcasting'. The Labour Party, university chancellors, a heavyweight battalion of clergy, Lord Reith and a posse of other peers all warned we were likely to go the way of America. There, they said, advertisers ruled programming and nothing (not even the Coronation!) had been spared their interruptions. In the long term, they may have been right, but during the 1950s they needn't have worried. Sir Kenneth Clarke's Independent Television Authority was in place to keep an eye on the ad-men, and in any case less than 200,000 sets were capable of receiving the first ITV broadcasts.

The commercials themselves – the very first was for Gibbs toothpaste – didn't prove much of a problem. People seemed to quite like them, but didn't go into any kind of shopping frenzy, and seemed more interested in the new channel's other novelty: entertaining programmes.

Along with the Coronation in 1953, ITV gave British television its biggest single boost of the decade, as competition forced programme makers to work for their viewers. Within two years, television licences outnumbered radio licences in Britain, and though the four regional ITV companies lost money for a while, they had moved solidly into profit by 1957.

Take Your Pick

Its remit only allowed ITV to show a few American programmes, but there was a distinctly transatlantic feel to the new channel's output. In its first week, ITV showed *I Love Lucy*, *Dragnet* and *Dr Kildare* from the USA, along with editions of *Double Your Money*, *Take Your Pick* and *Opportunity Knocks*, all American formats with reduced prizes. Early home-grown attractions included *Emergency Ward 10*, *The Adventures of Robin Hood* and the perennial *Sunday Night At The London Palladium*.

News programmes from ITN made a particular splash. In contrast to the

The Princess and the Equerry

For two years from 1955, the nation was more or less gripped by the doomed romance, originally revealed by the foreign press, between Princess Margaret and an equerry, divorced war hero Group Captain Peter Townsend. On the basis of that divorce, and remembering Wallace Simpson, the royal family closed ranks, aided by a cabinet containing three divorced ministers and, in Eden, a divorced PM. The 18th century Royal Marriages Act was invoked, Townsend was packed off to Brussels and Margaret left to await her 25th birthday, when the Act lost its force. Townsend impressed press and public with his gentlemanly behaviour throughout, but peer pressure told on Margaret, who eventually announced the end of the affair as her 'duty to the Commonwealth'. Margaret later earned a reputation as an unconventional royal, sealed it by her choice of companions, and eventually married a photographer, Anthony Snowden. A few years and royal divorces down the line, who would have denied her the Group Captain?

BBC's bland, impersonal broadcasts, they showed the audience its newsreaders, called them 'newscasters', and let them express their personalities. Presenters such as Christopher Chataway, Robin Day and Ludovic Kennedy seized the opportunity to spice up the genre and become celebrities in their own right.

This was all quite a shock to the BBC, which had promised to maintain standards in the face of commercial TV, but had already started competing with it. A plethora of new BBC shows arrived that summer, including *Life with the Lyons*, *Dixon of Dock Green*, *This is Your Life*, *The Brains Trust*, *The Woodentops* and *Crackerjack* – but the strategy didn't really work. Most people agreed the BBC made better programmes, but they still watched ITV. By 1958, when ITV enjoyed a 70 percent share of the audience, questions were being asked about the need for a licence fee if no-one was watching.

Family Favourites

On the evening of the ITV launch, the BBC Light Programme ran an episode of *The Archers* in which Grace Archer was killed – and it stole the headlines next morning. Radio was still enjoying what many see as its golden age, and was still big news in Britain.

There were other stations on the dial, Radio Luxembourg in particular, but the BBC essentially had radio to itself in 1955. It offered listeners a choice of three networks: the Home Service, the Light Programme and, since the late 1940s, the arts-based Third Programme. Between them they provided a varied soundtrack to home and work life, and could attract audiences of up to 20 million.

On Saturday mornings, Uncle Mac's 'Hello, children everywhere' signalled the start of Children's Favourites, while on weekdays *Listen With Mother* ('Are you sitting comfortably? Then I'll begin') filled the morning slot and *Children's Hour* was on every afternoon. Older listeners could enjoy science-fiction, with *Journey Into Space*, or the spine-chilling horror of *Appointment With Fear*, but were more likely to gather round one of the serials, *Mrs Dale's Diary* or, of course, *The Archers*.

Tony Hancock – a comic genius eventually blown away by the self-disgust that created his pompous, ignorant and dearly beloved Sage of East Cheam.

Alongside *The Goon Show*, *Hancock's Half Hour* was the nation's favourite comedy, but *Meet The Huggets*, *Educating Archie* and *Take It From Here* were all popular. Jean Metcalfe introduced *Woman's Hour* every day, and *Gardeners' Question Time* was always presented by Fred Loads, Bill Sowerbutts and Alan Gemmel.

Two-Way Family Favourites, the BBC's way of keeping servicemen abroad in touch with home, announced the time at noon each Sunday, and in the afternoon *Down Your Way* toured the nation for a bit of a chat with the locals. Wilfred Pickles was also out and about inviting ordinary folk to *Have A Go*, a show that had more fans than anything else on the air.

Shows dedicated solely to music were, however, comparatively rare. *Concert Hour*, *Henry Hall's Guest Night* and *Billy Cotton's Band Show* all mixed music and light comedy, and Roy Plomley's *Desert Island Discs* was really a conversation. No such distractions were permitted in *Music While You Work*, and *Housewives' Choice* played largely requests, but the first show dedicated to hit records – *Pick of The Pops*, presented by Franklin Engelmann – was only just starting out in 1955.

All Change Upstairs

Both the main political parties bade farewell to popular and successful leaders in 1955. Winston Churchill finally retired as Prime Minister in April, turning down the last dukedom offered to a commoner, and handed over to Foreign Secretary Anthony Eden. With such a modest majority, Eden had little choice but to call an immediate election, and it took place on 29 May, giving Chancellor 'Rab' Butler just enough time to produce a vote-catching budget.

Attlee, Labour's leader since 1935, set off on his traditional tour of the country, and even appeared once on television but, at 77, he came across as a tired figure. His party was visibly split, with Nye Bevan still in the wilderness and the left still demanding sweeping nationalisation, so Labour took on the electorate without a clear platform, and paid the price. In what was later seen as the dullest election of modern times, the Conservatives increased their overall majority to 60 in a slightly larger Commons, while Labour lost another 18 seats and the Liberals stayed stuck on six. Now Attlee retired, to be replaced by Hugh Gaitskell in September. Gaitskell inherited a noisy TUC campaign to introduce the 40-hour week, and mounting exasperation with unions in a year marked by major dock and rail strikes. He would never find a way to reconcile the two wings of his party, and was still leading the Opposition when he died in 1963. Meanwhile Eden, after years in waiting while Churchill clung to office, would not have long to enjoy his victory.

Bertrand Russell – philosopher, mathematician and acknowledged Brain of Britain – speaks at his 'peace meeting' in July. An internationally respected figure since the 1920s, and never afraid of public debate, Russell was appalled by nuclear proliferation, a view shared by his counterpart in the realm of physics, Albert Einstein.

Disarm or Deter?

Enthusiastic consumerism rather assumed the world wasn't about to end, a view some highly eminent scientists were doing their best to undermine in 1955. Bertrand Russell and Albert Einstein, who died later that year, came out with the July Manifesto, calling for nuclear disarmament, and 52 Nobel prizewinners signed another petition to the same effect. More such dissident protests would follow. Albert Schweitzer issued a personal appeal for disarmament in 1956, and 9,000 scientists presented a petition to the UN in 1958, but they cut little ice with the relevant governments.

There was a moment when it looked as if the superpowers might begin disarming. The USSR suggested a 75 percent arms cut, and Eisenhower responded with his 'open skies' initiative, which would have allowed each side to monitor the other from the air. A summit was arranged in Geneva for July, between Eisenhower, Eden, French president Edgar Faure and Khrushchev, now established as Soviet leader, and the Cold War went cool for a few weeks. In fact, little of substance emerged from the superpowers' first summit since Potsdam, ten years earlier. Both sides backed away from arms reduction, and Khrushchev turned down open skies, recognising that Russia had more secrets to lose. By November,

OTHER NEWS...

... 23 January, Sutton Coldfield train crash kills 23 and injures 43... Soviet premier Malenkov replaced by Nikolai Bulganin.... Jazz legend Charlie Parker dies at 34... Anglo-Pakstani Roy Smith plays for Portsmouth... basic income tax reduced... the Warsaw Pact is signed in May... Newcastle's third FA Cup in five years, and their last to date... Chelsea win the title, ruining all the jokes about them... dock strike begins, 23 May... Daily Mail royal insider 'Crawfie' comes unstuck after strikes postpone Ascot, but her pre-written report still appears... Jimmy Young at No. 1 with *Unchained Melody* in June... hurricane in Granada wipes out almost half the world's nutmeg crop... *Waiting For Godot* goes over weird in London.... fluoridation of water supplies begins... Coca Cola copyrights the name 'Coke'... Chuck Berry records *Maybellene* ... US occupation of Japan ends... Tolkien completes *The Lord of the Rings* ...the first Guinness Book of Records is published... black American teenager Emmett Till is abducted from his uncle's home after allegedly whistling at a white woman; authorities find his body three days later... 82 die in Le Mans disaster... acupuncture is introduced to the West... UK's record 24-hour rainfall total, 279 mm, at Martinstown, near Dorchester, in July... Donald Campbell sets new world water-speed record at 202 mph... the first white composite tooth fillings... Gordon Pirie beats Emil Zatopek over 10,000 metres... trouble flares on the Israel-Jordan border... first suggestion that Shakespeare and Marlowe were the same man... Juan Péron is overthrown by Argentine military coup in September... Dali's *The Lord's Supper*... Eisenhower suffers a heart attack in late September, and Wall Street plummets.... David Ben-Gurion returns from retirement to be Israeli premier... general strike in Cyprus against British control on 29 September... Dr Jonas Salk announces the success of his polio vaccine... 20 November, 10 dead and 99 hurt in Didcot train crash... goodbye: Albert Einstein, Alexander Fleming, Thomas Mann....

when Khrushchev used the unfortunate phrase 'we will bury you' about economic competition with the West, the brief respite from Cold War tension was over.

Sister Rosa

On 1 December, in Montgomery, Alabama, a 40 year-old black seamstress on her way home from work was told by a bus driver to give up her seat to a white passenger. Despite local race laws, Mrs Rosa Parks refused and was turned off the bus. Black people then boycotted the city buses in a peaceful protest that lasted until the law was overturned a year later. It was the first great campaign of what would soon become a nationwide civil rights movement in America, and it made the name of its leader, the Reverend Dr Martin Luther King.

Racial equality was a simmering and divisive issue throughout the decade in the USA, in the north as well as in the conservative southern states. Punctuated by terrible crimes of violence, especially by the white supremacist Ku Klux Klan, the civil rights movement generated a wealth of African-American protest literature and, in Dr King, a gentle and globally admired father figure, who would later become its greatest martyr.

The Reverend Martin Luther King Jr, pastor of the Dexter Avenue Baptist Church in Montgomery, Alabama. Still in his mid-twenties, King would soon make global headlines with his campaign for racial equality through peaceful protest.

Final Judgment

Call girl, divorcee and mother of two Ruth Ellis was tried at the Old Bailey in June 1955 for what might be called a crime of passion. In April, she had emptied a gun into her boyfriend, racing driver David Blakely, after discovering his infidelity. Though Blakely had clearly mistreated her, there was no doubt about the deed, and she was sentenced to death for murder. For three weeks the Home Office was bombarded by petitions and protests demanding commutation, as the country erupted into a fierce debate about capital punishment. Was hanging only applicable to certain murders? Was it wrong altogether? Was it wrong to execute a woman? Was it wrong to ask another human being to perform an execution? None of this helped Ruth Ellis, who was hanged by executioner Albert Pierrepoint at Holloway Prison on 13 July, but nobody has been executed under British law since.

Ruth Ellis was a rather foolish young woman, struggling on the fringes of glamour, wealth and crime. They did not treat her kindly, and the fact that she was clearly a victim as well as a killer won a lot of public sympathy.

Kaboom!

If history fitted neatly into the calendar, a year like 1956, with 'turning point' written all over it, would have been the beginning of a new decade, or even a new century.

Rationing was by now a fairly distant memory, and economists talked of a breakthrough in what they were calling 'upper-working class' spending power. Scientists promised electricity 'too cheap to meter', as the world's first commercial nuclear reactor came on stream at Calder Hall in Cumbria. Sociologists welcomed changing consumer habits, as the number of new-fangled supermarkets topped

Elvis struts his stuff on stage in '56, his greatest year. How he got his legs into that position remains a mystery, but the girls seemed to like it anyway.

3,000 and television's appeal cut cinema audiences in half. Culture vultures were meanwhile announcing the birth of a new wave with John Osborne's play *Look Back In Anger*, which opened at the Royal Court in May.

The Pelvis

Elvis made his records and performed his gyrations in the far distant USA, but he was on the UK charts just a few weeks after his American debut with *Heartbreak Hotel*.

It's hard to say exactly what made Elvis Aaron Presley, a singing, dancing truck driver from Tennessee, the perfect embodiment of rock'n'roll. The voice, the look, the hips, the songs and the times all had something to do with it. So did the colour of his skin. Black artists had been bumping and grinding for years, but it still took a white face to really move the markets. Fats Domino and Little Richard followed Elvis into the British charts later in the year, but it would be almost a decade before black performers could enjoy the full benefit of their talents.

Whatever magic Elvis was working that year, it was potent stuff. *Heartbreak Hotel* entered the UK Top Twenty on 11 May, and by the time it dropped out in October, *Hound Dog* and *Blue Suede Shoes* were carrying the torch. Elvis was never off the charts for the rest of the decade, and was without doubt the most famous man in the world by the end of the year.

Putting On The Style

Skiffle and its undisputed king, Lonnie Donegan, are often overlooked when it comes to the foundations of British pop. Britain's DIY version of rock'n'roll was a cheery hybrid of 'talking' blues, 20s jug band music and strictly low budget instrumentation. It was already popular at the start of 1956, and prospered for a couple of years afterwards.

The bands typically featured a double bass (perhaps made from a broom handle and tea chest), a kazoo or three, a washboard and as many 'rhythm' guitars as possible. Skiffle was easy to play, lively enough for dancing, cheap enough for almost anyone to have a go, and filled an important creative gap while the nation's youth found a way to get hold of electric guitars.

Rebels With A Clause

Elvis was in movies before 1956 was out, as *Love Me Tender* became one of six rock'n'roll films that year. He would prove a lot less rebellious than he looked, especially after he was drafted and trained to be a family entertainer. Most 50s pop stars followed his example and opted for rapid absorption by the powers of conventional showbiz, especially in Britain, where the pattern was set by the nation's very first rocker, Tommy Steele.

British teenagers had to work hard for a fix of rock'n'roll. BBC radio almost never played it and though television was making a start with *Six-Five Special*, it was hardly cutting edge stuff. Pubs were forbidden and didn't do that sort of music, clubs didn't exist for the young, and the occasional concert was likely to be trad jazz or, at best, skiffle. That left Radio Luxembourg's lousy reception, listening booths at record shops, and juke boxes. The places to hear juke boxes were coffee bars, and they became the gathering points for a generation of expresso-drinking, music-mad teenagers.

Coffee bars were also good places for an aspiring singer to strum his stuff. That's how Tommy Hicks, an impish young merchant seaman from Bermondsey, came to be discovered, renamed, and foisted on the nation. Steele's unforgettable *Rockin' With The Caveman* made the top ten that autumn, and he followed up with a string of light rock hits during the next year or so. By 1958 he was an unashamed song and dance man, releasing ballads or novelty songs, and appealing to mums in a series of 'cheeky chappy' film roles.

The Riviera Touch

New styles and sex symbols had shaken, but not overthrown, contemporary fashion's love affair with long-gloved, fine-boned sophistication. Personified in Britain by the glacial Barbara Goalen, and by American model Suzy Parker, high style still dominated the glossy world of catwalks and magazine covers. Though she had strong competition from the likes of Deborah Kerr, Ingrid Bergman, Katherine Hepburn and Vivien Leigh, Hollywood's acknowledged queen of sophistication was Grace Kelly.

Tommy Steele soon gave up hanging out in coffee bars like this, even for the sake of a good publicity shot.

Kelly's career was at its peak in 1956. She starred as the epitome of cool, moneyed chic in *Rear Window*, and alongside William Holden in *The Bridges at Toko-Ri*. On 19 April, image became reality when she retired from movies and married Prince Rainier Grimaldi III of Monaco. It was the showbiz wedding of the decade, perhaps of the century, but for Her Serene Highness Princess Grace it meant life under a spotlight more focused than anything in Hollywood, where so many other stars vied for attention.

The French were thrilled to find Grace Kelly on their doorstep, but were even more excited about Brigitte Bardot, whose fame went global with the release of Roger Vadim's *And God Created Woman*. Bardot went on to redefine lifestyle options for young women, especially in France, where her rather chauvinist attitude to sex became a national obsession. Bardot's friends and lovers became French, even international, stars in her wake, and she almost single-handedly turned the hitherto sleepy port of Saint Tropez into a jet-set playground.

The Adventures of Nikita, Part One

How dangerous was the Soviet Union and what were its aims? These questions had been on hold since Stalin's death in 1953, but by now the succession had clearly devolved on Nikita Khrushchev.

Brigitte Bardot shines her light on fellow actress Isabelle Corey at Cannes. Set alongside Grace Kelly and Marilyn Monroe, Bardot's wilful, emancipated nymphet was an altogether more challenging sex symbol.

Khrushchev, who would denounce Stalin at that summer's 20th Party Congress, seemed a relatively moderate proposition at first. Amid rumours that Soviet citizens were enjoying a little more personal liberty, he mended fences with Tito and settled a long-running dispute with Albania. He met Eisenhower at Geneva, he made overtures to nationalist groups in Warsaw Pact countries and, in April 1956, he made an official trip to the UK.

Khrushchev arrived at Portsmouth by battle-cruiser, met Prime Minister Anthony Eden at Chequers and paid the Queen a visit, coming across like a jovial tourist in a series of staged photo and newsreel opportunities. The only serious trouble he encountered came, predictably enough, from British socialists, who blamed Russia for giving their ideology a bad name.

At a dinner with the parliamentary Labour Party, Khrushchev found himself barracked and asked a series of belligerent questions about civil rights. George Brown was particularly aggressive, but Nye Bevan and Hugh Gaitskell weren't far behind. A bewildered Khrushchev kept smiling afterwards, though he later admitted he had never met socialists quite like the British Labour Party.

By the end of the year Khrushchev's bonhomie was well and truly forgotten, as he set about bringing Eastern Europe into line. In the autumn, tanks went into Poland to stifle anti-Soviet riots, and a much bigger revolt erupted in Hungary a few days later. On 23 October, 200,000 protesters in Budapest released imprisoned nationalist leader Imre Nagy and installed him as premier. After much soul-searching inside the Kremlin, Red Army forces entered Budapest in early November and quelled the uprising after three days of fighting. Three thousand Russians and 7,000 Hungarians died. Nagy, who was promised safe conduct, was later executed.

Non-Communist governments reacted with shock, protest and little else, though the British did cancel a Royal Ballet visit to Moscow. Despite public pressure there wasn't much they could do, short of risking all-out war, not likely in a US election year, let alone in the middle of the Suez Crisis.

Rock Years

Mythology is the enemy of hindsight, and our image of the Rock 'n' Roll Age is a myth. For all its massive impact, the Elvis phenomenon didn't really secure the future of rock 'n' roll, but instead opened the floodgates to teenage music of all sorts. Rock'n'roll stuck around for the rest of the decade, and has never quite gone away, but within a year or so it was just one component in an expanding market. Teenage consumers could be loyal (ask any Elvis fan), but were generally a lot more fickle than their elders. Stars and styles began to come and go more quickly, and kids were soon spending their money on sugary teen pop, skiffle, novelty hits or whatever else took their fancy. Meanwhile, despite their dismissal from history at the moment Elvis arrived, crooners and tune-smiths would keep churning out the hits, quietly outselling rockers and pop stars right up to the end of the decade.

The Empire Strikes... back you come, lads!

Anthony Eden had negotiated Britain's 1954 agreement with Egypt despite a storm of protest from the Suez Group of MPs, led by the forensic oratory of Enoch Powell. The group insisted that Britain keep control of the Canal, but also that America was trying to undermine British imperial influence all over the globe. The group's fury knew no bounds when, a matter of days after planned British troop withdrawals were completed in July 1956, Nasser broke the agreement by nationalising the Canal.

Nasser was retaliating against the removal of Anglo-American Aswan Dam loans, a knock-on from Egypt's recognition of Communist China in April, but the highly strung Eden felt personally betrayed and reacted accordingly. Some newspapers were already calling him a weak successor to Churchill, and his deportation of Cypriot nationalist Archbishop Makarios hadn't stopped them, so he felt bound to fight back.

Eden had strong support in the cabinet, especially from Harold Macmillan, and even stronger backing from the French, who had their own grievances over Nasser's funding of Algerian rebels. But the support expected from the Americans never

materialised. Instead, Eisenhower publicly announced his opposition to punitive action against Egypt, and a United Nations resolution forbade it. Despite British protests, Dulles remained obdurate, and arranged peace talks in London that dragged on fruitlessly into October.

By then, a timetable had been agreed between the Israelis, the French and the British for a

Early November in Trafalgar Square – as British troops invade Egypt in defiance of the UN, protesters make their feelings clear. In the event it was America's attitude, not popular protests or UN resolutions, which made the difference between war and peace.

coordinated invasion of Egypt. Israel launched a completely successful attack across Sinai on 29 October, and Anglo-French forces were set in motion next day. In London, the government was facing a rising tide of popular opinion against what looked like an act of old-fashioned imperial greed, but its real problem was a run on Sterling, brought about by withdrawal of American financial support.

The invasion had advanced 25 miles down the Canal, with 50 dead and some 300 Egyptians killed, when Eden called it off on 6 November. The entire episode was expensive, humiliating and counter-productive. The Canal had been blocked by hulk ships, which had been inadvertently bombed into position by the RAF, and Britain was unable to use it for some time. The Aswan Dam was eventually built with Russian money, and Nasser was confirmed as an Arab hero. Eden was derided on all sides for having gone so far, only to back down, and he suffered a breakdown. He withdrew to Jamaica for recuperation, leaving Rab Butler to run the country, but never returned to full-time work and resigned early the following year. Even more significantly, Washington decided it must treat the Middle East as yet another frontier against Communism and began to get seriously involved.

The Lucky Country

There was a place, English-speaking and ruled by the Queen, where it seemed the tensions of the Cold War could be forgotten, the long summers were always warm and a future of secure plenty seemed assured. Things were looking pretty good for Australia in the mid-1950s.

Once a place to be sent, Australia had become the place to go and build a new life. With a tiny population occupying an enormous land mass, it had immigration agreements with many European nations, but was especially anxious to recruit from the mother country. Sponsored community schemes such as 'Bring Out a Briton' had helped persuade more than a million people to sail south from the UK since the War, many of them 'Ten Pound Poms', named after the boat fare they were offered as an incentive. By late 1956, Australian cities were rapidly catching up with European standards of living, and British self-esteem was at its lowest ebb. There could have been no better time to showpiece life in the 'lucky country' and, as luck would have

This is Betty, from Scotland, in 1956. She's off with her parents for a long sea voyage and a new life in Melbourne, Australia. Millions of Europeans had already been drawn south by well-aimed marketing campaigns.

it, no better shop window than the Melbourne Olympics.

For a start, the Olympics glorified the thing Australia was best at – sport. You couldn't move for Australian sporting success stories. They had long held the whip hand in cricket, but now Australians dominated international men's tennis, with Lew Hoad and Ken Rosewall vying for individual supremacy and the Davis Cup team almost invincible. Golfer Peter Thompson won three consecutive British Opens, and racing driver Jack Brabham took three Grand Prix world titles. Bush-raised miler Herb Elliott made himself the world's best, sprinter Betty Cuthbert was equally dominant, and swimmer Dawn Fraser would hold the Olympic freestyle title until the 1972 Games.

Almost 3,200 athletes took part in the Games, compared with almost 5,000 at Helsinki in 1952, but it was a long journey and half a dozen boycotts were in progress. The event was a success anyway, though politics did intrude when a water polo match between Hungary and the USSR got out of hand. Australia came a good third, behind the two superpowers, and the British did well, bringing home 24 medals, six of them gold.

Dream Machine

The government came up with a new way to make a little money on the side in 1956, when it introduced Premium Bonds, the first national lottery and a smart form of virtually interest-free government borrowing. At the same time it unveiled ERNIE (the Electronic Random Number Indicator). A cheat-proof machine designed to pick winning bonds in the monthly draw, ERNIE could win you a first prize of £1,000. This was hardly the stuff of dreams, even after it had been hastily raised to £5,000, but a lot of 50s babies would come into the world armed with a few bonds as gifts from relatives and well-wishers. ERNIE's top prizes grew steadily, but would never keep up with Britain's number one dream tickets, the football pools, which were already offering a staggering £75,000 top prize, and turned their lucky few big winners into instant, if fleeting, celebrities.

This 1956 equivalent of a lottery booth attracted plenty of customers outside the Royal Exchange on 1 November, the day premium bonds became available. After all, even a top prize of a thousand pounds was more than most people earned in a year.

OTHER NEWS...

Britain sends 1,600 paratroops to Cyprus in January... in February, Guy Burgess and Donald Maclean appear on a Soviet newsreel... 16 February, British MPs vote for abolition of the death penalty... Dean Martin at No 1 with *Memories Are Made of This*... Pakistan declares itself the first Islamic republic, but stays in the Commonwealth... Tunisia gains independence from France in March, France also grants Morocco independence... Ingmar Bergman wins world fame with *The Seventh Seal*.... Yul Brynner best actor, Ingrid Bergman, best actress... UK bank rates reach 5.5%, the highest since 1932.... Velcro appears on the scene, as does the pager... charts expand to top thirty... Gold Coast, later known as Ghana, becomes independent.... British Railways abolishes 3rd class travel on 4 June... half a million French troops are stationed in Algeria by June... House of Lords rejects bill abolishing the death penalty... in June, Marilyn Monroe marries the playwright Arthur Miller... Jim Laker takes 9-37 and 10-53 to rout the Australians at Old Trafford... IBM creates the first hard disk drive.... Granada, ATV and ABC all start broadcasting... the first transatlantic telephone calls by submarine cable... the top half of Elvis performs on *The Ed Sullivan Show* in September... the RAF retires its last Lancaster bomber... Richard Hamilton's This Is Tomorrow exhibition is called 'pop art'... Eisenhower is re-elected president, Democrat Adlai Stevenson again defeated.... in November, a new transmitter at Emley Moor, Yorkshire, brings ITV to 5 million more viewers... the first African killer bees are imported from South Africa to Brazil... *Peyton Place* by Grace Metalious, steams up the bestseller lists... Rocky Marciano retires in April, undefeated after 49 bouts... Japan joins the UN... the US Supreme Court outlaws racial segregation on public transport.... Fats Domino, Carl Perkins, Little Richard, Frankie Lymon and the Teenagers and Gene Vincent make UK chart debuts... petrol rationed in Britain ...Rose Heilbron is Britain's first female judge...goodbye: Bertold Brecht, Tommy Dorsey, Bela Lugosi, Walter de la Mare, Jackson Pollock, Art Tatum...

Fallout

After the thrills and spills of the previous year, 1957 was a year of consolidation and recovery. Social fads settled down to become accepted standards, and the country coped with the painful after-effects of Suez.

There was no revenge for the humiliating climbdown of the previous autumn, only repercussions. Eden resigned in January, but Chancellor Harold Macmillan nipped any talk of an early election in the bud when he made the short move to Number 10. Macmillan had been a strong supporter of the Suez adventure, but would treat the Empire more gracefully from now on.

The process of 'decolonisation' was now in full flow. Britain paid its tolls to the Egyptian government like everyone else when the Canal reopened for business in April, by which time the mandates of Gold Coast and Togoland had become the independent state of Ghana. Malaya became a sovereign state in the summer, and independence would soon be granted to trouble spots Cyprus and Singapore.

All this didn't quite undermine Britain's sense of its own global importance. In March, the Treaty of Rome established the European Economic Community, joining France, Germany, Belgium, Holland, Luxembourg and Italy in a common market. Britain kept its traditional distance from the continent, preferring to tie its destiny to special relationships with the US and the Commonwealth. Soon afterwards, on 15 May, Britain's much-vaunted 'independent deterrent'

Manchester University's giant radio telescope at Jodrell Bank, Cheshire, was the most powerful in the world, but was in deep financial trouble by the time it was completed. Intended purely as an astronomical tool, the telescope was saved by the outbreak of the space race, as American and Russian agencies hired it to track long-range spacecraft.

mushroomed once more in the slipstream of the superpowers, when Britain exploded its first hydrogen bomb on Christmas Island in the Indian Ocean.

The Minister's New Clothes

Would America start a world war to protect western Europe? The question lay behind Britain's decision to develop its own nuclear weapons, and the H-bomb was greeted by both sides of parliament, along with much of the press, as a vital boost to national defence. Even Labour's most famous 'disarmer' agreed. 'Do not send the British foreign minister naked into the international conference chamber', Aneurin Bevan implored that year's Party conference, and the phrase came to symbolise the H-bomb's equation with global clout. After all, the USA and the Soviet Union were the only other powers with H-bombs.

It would soon become clear that Britain couldn't compete with superpower defence budgets, but if the H-bomb failed to revive the old *pax britannica*, it certainly breathed life into the nation's anti-nuclear movement. Even before the new bomb was exploded, British quaker Harold Steele and his wife made headlines by setting off on a suicide voyage into the test area as a protest against the weapon. Thoroughly lampooned by a jingoistic popular press, 'H-Bomb Harold' reached Tokyo to discover that the test had already taken place, but better organised protests were to follow.

Queen and Country

There was plenty more to complain about that spring. A wave of strikes hit the country in March, bringing stoppages on the railways, and the Suez Canal's prolonged closure brought a return of petrol rationing. The motor trade was in relatively rude health, with British designs doing well abroad, but buyers still faced long waiting lists and the problems of road congestion were already a national talking point. Even this didn't stop the usual rush to the coast by Easter holidaymakers, but they had less to spend as the bank rate reached a record seven percent during another balance of payments crisis.

A touch of national grumpiness began to take some of the shine off the royal family. The end of the affair for Margaret and Peter Townsend brought a few mutterings about Her Majesty's cold heart, but an editorial in the generally low-profile *National and English Review* went further, accusing the Queen of lacking both personality and a sufficiently broad education. Later in the year, just before Elizabeth's official visit to Washington, Malcolm Muggeridge raised a storm in America with an article entitled 'Does England Really Need A Queen?' Straw polls in the newspapers suggested that many subjects agreed with criticisms levelled at the royals, but that didn't stop a furious backlash from some of those who didn't.

Loyal support came from all classes and in many forms. Lord Altrincham, the *Review's* editor, was attacked by fellow aristocrats, by the Archbishop of Canterbury and, physically, by the League of Empire Loyalists. Muggeridge had his home vandalised, lost all his BBC work, and was dropped from the *Sunday Dispatch*. Playwright John Osbourne, who had called the monarchy the 'gold filling in a mouth of decay', didn't suffer any such career setbacks. He didn't need anyone's approval, because he was officially angry.

White Heat

Kingsley Amis had hinted at it with *Lucky Jim*, and John Osbourne himself had given it a focus in Jimmy Porter, the public school dropout of his 1956 play *Look Back In Anger*. By 1957, when John Braine's rough-edged social climber, Joe Lampton, made his debut in *Room At The Top*,

From the left, Mary Ure, Alan Bates, Helena Hughes and Kenneth Haigh in John Osbourne's *Look Back in Anger*, a few weeks into its opening run at the Royal Court. The work of 'angry young men' made stars of many writers and performers, and created fictional characters that became household names, but didn't do much for women on any level.

Hero of the beat generation and indisputably the coolest man on the planet, trumpeter Miles Davis trades licks with saxophonist Sonny Rollins at the New York Jazz Festival.

it had happened. They had all become part of a literary movement – the Angry Young Men.

Novelists Stan Barstow, Alan Sillitoe and Keith Waterhouse would all become senior members of the gang in the next two years, but it was already the end of the road for one of the earliest and angriest of the breed, Colin Wilson. Wilson, a self-educated dabbler in homespun philosophy, had become a star at 24 in 1955, when his debut novel, *The Outsider*, was greeted by British critics as a masterpiece. His second, *Religion and the Rebel*, sparked precisely the opposite reaction in 1957.

Angry Young Men, if they could be classified together at all, wrote about misfits battling their way to fulfilment against the 'Establishment', and attacked their targets with much more passion than British audiences had been used to. The literary establishment was predictably unimpressed, the public preferred *From Russia With Love*, *The Guns of Navarrone* or *On The Beach*, and the writers themselves denied that they were part of a movement. Even the critics soon dropped the label, but the Angry Young Men did blaze a trail for the next generation to explore issues of sex and class. None would do so more powerfully than Harold Pinter, whose first play, *The Room*, opened in 1957.

American misfits were getting literary representation from a group of writers known as The Beats. Depending on your viewpoint, the Beats either rejected material slavery and wandered among the free, or dropped out of middle-class backgrounds for just long enough to write about it and develop various addictions. Their bible was Jack Kerouac's 1957 debut novel *On The Road*, William Burroughs was their chieftain and their poet laureate was Allen Ginsburg. They dug a lot of jazz, cool stuff like Miles Davis and Thelonius Monk, and spoke a lot of 'jive'. They were cats or chicks who got very drunk and smoked 'jazz woodbines'. Things were either groovy or square, and square bugged them so much they sometimes flipped. They were among the first white American kids self-consciously pretending to be black, and their self-appointed chronicler, Norman Mailer, called them 'white niggers'.

The British Are Coming

The success of plays such as *Look Back In Anger* and Arnold Wesker's *Roots*, bred a new kind of stage star in the late 1950s. After decades of being smothered by the media, provincial accents were suddenly all the rage, along with performers such as Albert Finney, Alan Bates, Kenneth Haigh, Tom Courtenay and Joan Plowright. In the 1960s they would add lustre to British film making – and it needed some, because although Britain boasted a small galaxy of Hollywood stars, headed by Lawrence Olivier and David Niven, the home industry lacked international crowd-pullers.

Apart from the national institution that was Margaret Rutherford, British movies relied on 'character actors' who were none too well known outside these shores. The one clear and ever-present exception was Alec Guinness. He enriched countless British films during the 1950s, including *The Horse's Mouth*, *The Man In The White Suit*, *The Ladykillers*, *Kind Hearts And Coronets* and many more of the industry's finest products. In 1957, his career peaked with an Oscar for his role in David Lean's *Bridge On The River Kwai*, which was the year's worldwide box office champion and went on to win seven other Oscars, including best film.

Scary Monsters

By 1957, the largely American sci-fi magazine industry had shrunk to a fraction of its size in the early 50s, but the great novels just kept coming. Among many others, masters of the genre were Isaac Asimov, Ray Bradbury, Arthur C. Clarke, Philip K. Dick, Robert A. Heinlein, Kurt Vonnegut Jr and John Wyndham, all at their peak. Wyndham, author of *Day of The Triffids*, *The Kraken Wakes* and *The Midwich Cuckoos*, was even British.

Science-fiction movies of the period have been accused of reflecting American paranoia about Communism, and many of them certainly featured laughable plots, but

A FASCINATING ADVENTURE INTO THE UNKNOWN!

EVERY HOUR HE GETS SMALLER...SMALLER...SMALLER... AND EVERY MOMENT THE TERROR MOUNTS!

THE INCREDIBLE **SHRINKING MAN**

A Universal International Picture starring

GRANT WILLIAMS · RANDY STUART

with APRIL KENT · PAUL LANGTON · RAYMOND BAILEY

Directed by JACK ARNOLD · Screenplay by RICHARD MATHESON · Produced by ALBERT ZUGSMITH

There we were, on the brink of a thousand technological frontiers, unsure of the powers we were unleashing or our fitness to handle them. How easily it could all go wrong. A contact with the wrong aliens, a tap into the wrong energy source or a key to the wrong scientific door, and humans might not feel so big anymore. No wonder sci-fi struck a chord with 50s audiences.

menacing aliens didn't have the field to themselves. It's true that, by 1957, Earth had survived *The Thing from Another World*, *The Beast from 20,000 Fathoms*, *The War of the Worlds*, *Godzilla*, *Them!* and, creepiest of all, *The Invasion of the Bodysnatchers*. On the other hand, *The Day the Earth Stood Still* had given us a friendly, caring alien in 1951, and *Forbidden Planet* had taken a shot at Shakespeare in space, while the big sci-fi hit of 1957 reflected another strong theme – fear of technology's mysteries – as a strange fog created *The Incredible Shrinking Man*.

Despite the local success of the BBC's *Quatermass* series, science-fiction was slow to make a real impact on television, though *The Twilight Zone* eventually pointed the way forward in 1959. Sci-fi fared rather better as radio entertainment, and gave Britain it's most upright space adventurer in *Dan Dare, Pilot of the Future*, who thrilled some of Radio Luxembourg's bigger audiences until 1956, graced *The Eagle* comic, and eventually became one of the less successful products of TV's sci-fi boom in the 60s.

Shock To The System

Popular interest in aliens, and a plague of UFO sightings in the later 50s, may have

had something to do with the imminent conquest of space, or at least the parts of it closest to Earth. The space age officially began on 4 October, when the Soviet Union launched the world's first artificial satellite, a metal ball, 23 inches across, called Sputnik. A month later Sputnik II went up, taking a dog called Laika on a one-way trip into orbit.

Sputnik wasn't much bigger than a beach ball, or much more exciting to look at, but its international impact was even more sensational than this dramatic image suggests.

The US government was absolutely horrified. It wasn't just that Russia had taken a clear lead at the cutting edge of modern technology. Sputnik, launched after America's Vanguard project had

Jimmy Young at his crooning peak, in 1952, riding camera for Gene Kelly on the set at Elstree studios. Not exactly Elvis, is he?

failed and before its Explorer project was ready, showed that the Soviets had a lead in rocket technology. That was a defence issue, because rockets were the key to making Intercontinental Ballistic Missiles work and, now that Surface-to-Air Missiles had made bombers so vulnerable, ICBMs were going to be the next big weapon.

America set about catching up in a hurry. On 7 November, just four days after Sputnik II's launch, Eisenhower appeared on television to announce a massive space programme, but the USA would not regain the lead until the 1960s. By 1959, Soviet rockets had brought dogs back to Earth in good condition, circled the Sun, and photographed the dark side of the Moon, while the Americans were still struggling to fire a rocket that could even reach the Moon.

Love a Duck?

One of Hollywood biggest hits in 1957, *The Sweet Smell Of Success*, made a British star of both the young Tony Curtis and his haircut. Not so long before, a man's haircut had just been a way of keeping tidy. Now, with Teddy Boys and all sorts of hybrid imitators strutting the streets, trendy young men sported genuine hairstyles, often quite extravagantly oiled and shaped. The Tony Curtis was 1957's hot style, but the basic and most common design was the DA, or Duck's Arse, named for the unmistakable physical resemblance but based on Elvis' hairstyle in 1956.

TTFN

Balladeer Jimmy Young enjoyed a string of hits in the early charts and two consecutive number ones in 1955, with *Unchained Melody* and *The Man from Laramie*. The hits dried up in 1957, so he tried for a career as a radio broadcaster. Beginning as the host of *Housewives Choice* on the Light Programme, he did some work for Radio Luxembourg before settling down to become a BBC disc jockey and political interviewer of considerable national stature.

Little Big Man

The 50s were great years for American oil tycoons, who made fabulous fortunes at minimal tax rates, but big players such as HL Hunt or S Richardson were faceless unknowns to the outside world. Then, in 1957, Britain discovered that the richest of them all was living and running his business in a suite at the London Ritz. The anonymity that had protected John Paul Getty, the world's wealthiest person with estimated assets of $1,000 million, was gone for ever. For a time, every discoverable detail of Getty's life was public business, from his extravagances in pursuit of women to his petty complaints over trivial expenses. Getty was soon driven out of the Ritz

Not Cheap, Just Nasty

Cheap electricity was supposed to be the bright side of nuclear development. Optimism was high in 1955, when the first civilian power station was opened in Cumbria, but the public was already being kept in the dark about various military establishments and about the possible dangers of nuclear reactors. The military plant at Windscale, also in remote Cumbria and now known as Sellafield, had been operational since 1950, but its existence was not made public until 1954, and it was still subject to heavy secrecy when it suffered a major nuclear accident in October 1957.

Human error allowed a reactor to catch fire when its fuel melted down. Procedural failure by fire-fighters new to nuclear accidents turned it into a blazing inferno that took three days to douse, and released large amounts of radioactive material into the atmosphere. No one was evacuated from the area while the fire blazed, and no warnings were given by the government of any special dangers or procedures to be followed. The main precaution taken after the event, as a radioactive cloud drifted southeast across Britain, was the destruction of milk from farms in the immediate area.

and into a Tudor mansion in Surrey, but he still couldn't retreat back into obscurity. He might have been rich as Croesus, but he was a reassuringly unattractive little man, and seemed satisfyingly miserable with all his money – the perfect tonic for grumpy Britain.

Alec Guinness on stage at the Golders Green Hippodrome. Britain gave the world a wealth of acting and film-making talent in the 50s, but we kept Alec Guinness for ourselves. With characteristic charm and modesty, he never really seemed to mind.

OTHER NEWS...

... Eden resigns on 9 January... February, Bill Haley and His Comets begin UK tour at the Dominion Theatre... the Duke of Edinburgh becomes a prince in February... JK Galbraith publishes *The Affluent Society*, a critique of consumerism... in April, plans to end conscription in 1960 are announced... US federal authorities begin a crackdown on the Mafia.... 'Sugar Ray' Robinson loses the world middleweight championship to Carmen Basilio... Israel hands the Gaza Strip over to UN authorities in March... Bermuda conference between Eisenhower and Macmillan... the USSR tests intercontinental ballistic missiles in August... there were 16 cities in the world with more than 1 million inhabitants in 1914; there are 71 in 1957... Francois 'Papa Doc' Duvalier becomes president of Haiti.... oral polio vaccine is introduced... Willy Brandt is elected mayor of West Berlin.... Professor Gordon Dobson of Oxford University discovers the ozone layer... *West Side Story* opens on Broadway... air-driven dental drill eases fillings... Everly Brothers release *Wake Up Little Susie*.... UK chart debuts for Andy Williams, Chuck Berry, Russ Conway, Jerry Lee Lewis, Paul Anka and Jackie Wilson... 'Busby Babes' of Manchester United miss out on the double, losing the Cup final to Aston Villa... Rangers and Falkirk share Scots honours... in September, the Woolfenden report recommends changes to UK homosexuality laws... Samuel Beckett's *Endgame* ... in October, the world's largest radio telescope is opened at Jodrell Bank, Cheshire... *Paths Of Glory*, *Twelve Angry Men*... women will now be admitted to the House of Lords... a third of married British women have jobs of some sort.... Buddy Holly and the Crickets at number one with *That'll Be The Day*... Nobel literature prize to Albert Camus... Harold Macmillan becomes the first British political leader to use an autocue in a broadcast from Number 10... annual advertising budgets in the UK now total £450 million, similar to the education budget... goodbye: Humphrey Bogart, Christian Dior, Oliver Hardy, Louis Mayer, Joe McCarthy, Charles Pathé, Diego Rivera, Dorothy Sayers, Jean Sibelius, Erich von Stroheim...

Building blocks

Meccano's 'miniature engineering for boys' had been one of the great toys for half a century, but the War had stopped production, and metal shortages had limited its comeback until the mid-50s. In 1958, a plastic toy building system arrived that was easier to use, cheaper, brighter and, above all, modern. Lego was here to stay. Meccano was given a makeover, so that sets had more parts and brighter colours, but it would always be old-fashioned from now on, and its mass-market days were numbered. Some of the world's political leaders were also playing with new kinds of building set in 1958, but they weren't all as good as Lego.

Shapes of Things

In the West Indies a new federation of islands came together at the start of the year, but had fallen apart by 1962. Nasser's pan-Arabic vision saw Egypt and Syria merged as the United Arab Republic, but that new system only lasted until 1961. Both did better than the Arab Union between Jordan and Iraq, which was built in May and torn down by an Iraqi nationalist coup in July. On the other hand, the new Common Market put together by West German leader Konrad Adenauer and French foreign minister Christian Pineau came into force on New Year's Day, and is still growing.

One criticism of 'The Six', heard regularly in Britain, was that the main function of Italy and the Benelux countries was to nurture German industry and French agriculture.

It took skill and patience to get creative with Meccano, and your dad was always better at it. By the late 50s, when convenience was king and parents were getting bewildered, kids were finding less stressful ways to build their fantasies.

Illustrated: No. 3 Outfit for 32/6d.

MECCANO
for Christmas
The Toy that grows with the Boy

Every boy enjoys making things with Meccano. And it is a wonderful way to learn, for Meccano teaches while it gives pleasure. Your boy will learn to think constructively as he plans new models. And he will learn to use his hands, too. He is building for the future . . . acquiring knowledge and creating something through his own skill. Give Meccano and let him learn this easy, most enjoyable way of all. You can start him with an Outfit for as little as 5/9d. and add to it as his knowledge grows.

This fine Dockside Crane is built with Outfit No. 6

MADE IN ENGLAND BY MECCANO LTD. BINNS RD., LIVERPOOL 13

Perhaps, but the Common Market was also about preventing further war and upheaval in Europe, and events across the Channel soon rammed that point home. In May, French colonial generals staged a *coup d'état* in Paris, and civil war seemed possible until the return from exile of Charles de Gaulle. De Gaulle became prime minister under a new constitution adopted, as the French Fifth Republic, on 1 June. He was elected president the following year, and would run France for another decade.

Though the crisis in Paris had abated by September, De Gaulle still had to deal with an empire in chaos and an economy in freefall. The year saw autonomy granted to French Guinea, Senegal, Gabon, Mauritania, Mali, the Central African Republic, Dahomey and the Ivory Coast, followed by a massive devaluation in December, when a hundred old francs became one new franc. No wonder the French were happy to deflect their energies into a new, optimistic partnership with the old enemy across the Rhine.

Never Never Land

Britain's post-Suez blues had just been a minor prang on the slow road to affluence, which became a dual carriageway in 1958 when the government dropped hire purchase restrictions. Free to live now, pay later, British consumers jumped at the chance, and four out of five households were on the 'never never' by the end of 1959, to a total tune of £1,000 million.

And why not, when you could get hold of a Ford Poplar for a downpayment of £4. 5s. 6p (£4.27), or take home a fridge for £3. 3s. 3p (£3.16). All the same, spending in advance could make an extra mouth to feed a bit of a problem, so it helped that the Church of England gave its approval to contraception in April, though it preferred the term 'family planning'.

A new type of 'fast breeder' had nothing to do with contraception or rabbits, but was a prototype nuclear reactor opened at Dounreay in the far north of Scotland. It was expected, but ultimately failed, to help make coal-mining redundant, and plans were unveiled in December to close 36 pits, beginning a process of modernisation that would reduce a once vital industry to insignificance.

Another invention destined to disappoint expectations was Christopher Cockerill's new hovercraft, publicly unveiled in May and touted as the writing on the wall for conventional ferries. The ferries are still running, and hovercraft never really developed beyond specialist uses and the short hop to Calais or Boulogne.

Amid all the tub-thumping and optimism surrounding the new invention, the ugliness and noisiness of the early Saunders-Roe production hovercraft was all but ignored.

Some pointers to the future did live up to the billing. Stereo records arrived and stayed, though the British wouldn't really get used to them for another decade, and parking meters, which reached London streets in July, have been multiplying ever since. The parking meter was never going to be a popular new gadget, but the LCC made sure by introducing it right in the middle of a seven-week London bus strike. As well as clogging the city's arteries with more cars, the strike forced permanent cuts in suburban Green Line services, from which they never fully recovered.

Other long-term winners introduced to the public in 1958 included children's TV institution *Blue Peter*, first broadcast by the BBC in October, and the world's first regular jet service to the USA, inaugurated once the Comet was back in the air. More people still steamed across the Atlantic than flew, but this was the last year that would be true, and steam was even losing out on British Railways, which introduced its last new smoke-belcher in 1958 and would stick to diesels or electric from now on.

Final Frontiers

The Earth, give or take the odd ocean trench, had just about been conquered by 1958, and at the start of the year Sir Edmund Hillary proved it. The hero of Everest had followed in Scott's footsteps, and in January became the first man to walk to the South Pole. Reactions were polite but muted. The fact that an American team had flown to the Pole and prepared for Hillary's arrival summed up the message – space was the place for explorers.

The USA got its first artificial satellite, Explorer I, into orbit at the end of January. Launched from Cape Canaveral, it weighed 31 lb (14 kg), making it a hundred times lighter than the third Sputnik, which went up later in the year. America redoubled its efforts, and NASA – the National Aeronautics and Space Administration – was founded in July to administer its challenge. More Explorers followed, along with a failed attempt at a moon-shot, but America's main contribution at this stage was discovery of the Van Allen belt, a band of radiation around the Earth that looked as if it might make the next stage of the race, human space travel, dangerous or impossible.

Peaceniks

It was common knowledge that Britain would have only four minutes to prepare if a nuclear attack came, compared with about 25 minutes in the USA, and nothing about government civil defence policy suggested it would be much help. Even the year's defence White Paper admitted there was 'at present no means

Police control queues at Tottenham Court Road tube station during the London bus strike. This kind of overcrowding on the Underground, considered shocking in 1958, would be a regular feature of London life by the end of the century.

of providing adequate protection... in the event of nuclear attack.' Some people, understandably enough, were frightened.

In February, popular fears coalesced with strands of political and professional doubt to form the Campaign for Nuclear Disarmament, or CND. Its first leaders were the stern dean of St Paul's, Canon John Collins, and no less a luminary than Bertrand Russell, while an all-star original executive included Michael Foot, JB Priestley, Benjamin Britten, EM Forster, Barbara Hepworth, Doris Lessing, Henry Moore, Edith Evans and Peggy Ashcroft. At its inaugural meeting, held in Westminster's Central Hall, a packed house heard AJP Taylor's critique of the H-bomb.

The first day of the first Aldermaston march, possibly the most cheerful mass protest of all time. This scene outside the Albert Memorial just about sums it up.

CND pulled off a major PR coup six weeks later, at Easter weekend, when it organised the first of many annual protest marches to the atomic weapons research facility at Aldermaston in Berkshire. No more than a couple of thousand protesters set off from Trafalgar Square on the Saturday, 5 April, for what would be a four-day journey, but a counter-demonstration in Hyde Park only attracted about 30 people.

The march won a lot more publicity than its numbers or behaviour merited. Newspapers, even the 'qualities', went around trying to interview Communists, but found very few, and the whole affair was extremely polite.

Aldermaston made both the CND logo and its 'ban the bomb' slogan nationally famous, and was the first of many annual marches, but it was ignored in the halls of power.

Black Britain

A regular carnival did not begin in the largely black enclave of Notting Hill until the mid-60s, but at August Bank Holiday its streets were already a lively celebration of Caribbean culture. West Indians had begun arriving during the late 1940s, but less than half a million non-white (or 'New Commonwealth') immigrants lived here by 1958. Most worked with the Post Office, the buses, the railways or the health service, in jobs for which they had been recruited during labour shortages. The routine discrimination they suffered was forced into the public eye when Teddy Boys went on the rampage in Notting Hill for three days over the 1958 Bank Holiday, attacking black people, sparking mass brawls and causing serious property damage. Smaller riots took place over the next few weekends, but public shock in the aftermath, along with tough sentences handed down to white rioters, put a stop to racial violence for a time. The problem would rear up with greater force in the 1960s.

Black Pearl

In the summer, a mixed race football team had come to the World Cup in Sweden, won it, and in the process made friends all over the world. Brazil would be every nation's second favourite team into the next century, and their teenage 'boy wonder', Edson Arantes do Nascimento, replaced Puskas as world football's greatest star. Better known by his childhood nickname, Pele, he scored twice in a 5-2 win.

Unless you're English, the tournament was Britain's best ever world cup, as all four home nations qualified for the last sixteen. Scotland went out in the first stage, as ever, and England were eliminated after a play-off with Russia, but both Northern Ireland and Wales made it to the quarter finals. The Irish were well beaten by the French and their scoring machine Juste Fontaine, but Wales performed heroically against the mighty Brazilians, before eventually going down one-nil.

Moderate international success that summer might have been no more than a postscript to a first English win in the European Cup, but Manchester United's genuine hopes in that tournament had died on the tarmac at Munich in February.

Munich

On 6 February, in Munich, a BEA Elizabethan airliner crashed in a blizzard on its third attempt at take-off. It was carrying Manchester United players and backroom staff, along with supporters and journalists, back from a European Cup tie, and 23 of the 43 passengers lost their lives, including seven United players. Manager Matt Busby and young Bobby Charlton both survived, although Busby was critically ill for a time, but England's greatest prospect, the brilliant 21 year-old Duncan Edwards, was among those killed.

The disaster's impact was multiplied by genuine popular affection for this particular young team, known as the 'Busby Babes'. Having almost won the 'double' the previous year, and performed with pioneering success in the European Cup, United

The 'Busby Babes' line up for the last time, before a bruising game with Red Star Belgrade that saw them qualify for the European Cup semi-final. From the left: **Edwards**, **Colman**, **Jones**, **Morgans, Charlton, Viollet, Taylor, Foulkes, Gregg, Scanlon, Byrne** [capt]. **Underlined players were among those killed at Munich.**

Six young debutantes, disguised as their mothers, arrive at Buckingham Palace for a spring presentation party. Next year, the Establishment marriage market would have to get by without royal patronage.

were expected to set new standards for club football, but when the remnant of the side returned to action, performances were understandably shaky. They still finished second in the league and reached the cup final, but the national wave of sympathy that followed them to Wembley couldn't prevent defeat at the hands of Nat Lofthouse and Bolton Wanderers.

Last Curtsey

By way of demonstrating that it was modern and in touch, Buckingham Palace had announced that royal presentation parties for debutantes would end after the 1958 season. The gesture to a more egalitarian society was generally applauded, but Britain's 'Debs' went right on performing work of national importance.

After Dior

Christian Dior had died in 1957, and it wasn't long before his dressy, impractical style went with him. Dior's acknowledged successor, Yves St. Laurent, exhibited a tribute to the master for his 1958 Paris show, featuring the Trapeze Line, but it was a last hurrah for the old ways. The success of Balenciaga's simple, comfortable 'sac' dress was already enabling high street shops to produce imitations for ordinary, fashion-conscious women, and in 1959 Laurent would put hemlines above the knee for the first time.

Mary Quant's simply decorated designs, often pinafore dresses, were meanwhile doing great business in the King's Road, a shopping street that was mutating into the home of the Chelsea Girl and a haven for trendy pleasure seekers. At the end of the decade Bazaar had a turnover of more than £200,000, and Quant was about to launch her clothes through a US chain.

Goodbye, Norah D

One minor news story of 1958 shed a wistful light on the passing of know-your-place, austerity Britain. Sir Bernard and Lady Norah Docker were reported to be selling her jewellery.

Sir Bernard had been chairman of Daimler when he married former dancer Norah Collins in the late 1940s, and they set about showing off their good fortune. Jewels, furs, cars, a mighty ocean-going yacht, extravagant parties… they became the image of conspicuous consumption and the antithesis of austerity, famous for making everyone else look poor.

Warbler in Wolf's Clothing

For a while, in the autumn, it looked as if British teens had at last found a real, live rock'n'roll icon of their own. Cliff Richard got his arrival just right. Elvis had joined the Army in April, and Tommy Steele was making records for parents, but Cliff still pouted, and even snarled, when he hit the charts in September. What was more, Cliff had a proper guitar band backing him up – The Drifters, who would soon become The Shadows – and Move It was the first proper rock'n'roll song ever made in Britain. Surely this was the real thing.

Within a year, Cliff was as safe as houses, topping the charts with Living Doll and Travellin' Light . By the early 1960s he was a fully established housewives' favourite, as well as a British film star, and went on to become Britian's most enduringly successful, and clean-living, family vocalist.

British teen music wouldn't get out from under Tin Pan Alley until the beat boom. In the meantime, it was stuck with showbiz priorities and some very silly names. Cliff, who was born Harry Webb, could have done worse in that respect, as could Terry Nelhams when he became Adam Faith in 1959, but it was harder to ignore the creative thinking behind names such as Marty Wilde, Billy Fury, Vince Eager or Johnny Gentle.

Lady Norah was a born celebrity, with a definite flare for publicity. For a time in 1951, while touring factories and schools in the manner of minor royalty, she rode around in a Daimler with gold-plated fittings, and she liked to hold champagne receptions for 'ordinary people' aboard the yacht. All this, and Norah's bejewelled

Nora Docker in her glory days, at the Oxford Union in 1954. On her left, Sir Bernard exudes his usual bemused tolerance, while Union President Michael Heseltine explains why he'll be sticking with that haircut for life.

appearances at every important social gathering, finally told on Sir Bernard's shareholders, who ousted him in 1956. Norah Docker's salad days were over, and the jewellery sale was the first clear sign of a decline in fortunes that saw the couple reduced to a bungalow in Jersey within a few years.

OTHER NEWS...

... Gibson 'flying V' guitar patented in January... Castro at large and waging 'total war' against the Batista regime in Cuba... Huw Wheldon's *Monitor* is televised in February; it will launch the careers of John Boormann, John Schlesinger and Ken Russell... David Niven wins best actor Oscar for *Separate Tables*... best picture is *Gigi*... at the movies: *Touch of Evil, Cat on a Hot Tin Roof, Vertigo, Attack of the 50-Foot Woman, The Fly, South Pacific*... global hula hoop craze begins.... Sidney Poitier becomes the first black Hollywood leading man in *The Defiant Ones*... Norwich City becomes the first third-division side to reach the FA Cup semi-final... war breaks out against British control of Aden in May, it will last until 1967... Alaska becomes the 49th US state.... C Northcote Parkinson states 'Parkinson's Law': work expands to fill the time available for its completion... *The Black and White Minstrel Show* is first shown in June... the US occupies the Lebanon to prevent a revolution by pro-Nasser Arabs in July... British troops enter Jordan in July to protect the monarchy... Ian Fleming's *Doctor No.*, Graham Greene's *Our Man In Havana*, Truman Capote's *Breakfast At Tiffany's*.... first edition of *Grandstand* in October.... *Wyatt Earp, Wells Fargo, Maverick* and *Wagon Train* are among more than 30 westerns being made for TV in Hollywood... Television Wales and West and Southern Television begin broadcasting... Cha Cha Cha is the year's dance craze for squares... bizarre telephone box 'cramming' craze reaches Britain from South Africa.... the silicon chip is invented... thalidomide is blamed for birth defects... Churchill finishes 4-volume *History of the English-speaking Peoples*.... in October, Pope Pius XII dies and John XXIII is elected... the first life peers are created... the Shell Building opens for business on the South Bank... the Civil Service accepts equal pay for women... Nasser's United Arab Republic gets loan from the USSR for the Aswan dam project in October... Soviet author Boris Pasternak wins the Nobel literature prize for *Doctor Zhivago*, but refuses it under state pressure... in December, radical CND protesters break into the US airbase at Swaffham, Norfolk and are jailed... goodbye: Malcolm Lockheed, Ralph Vaughan Williams, Harry M. Warner...

Here comes summer?

Years that end with a '9' tend to encourage a sense of history. People look back at the decade just passed, and forward to what Anthony Eden called the 'perils and promise' of a new age. Had Britain come through the 50s in good shape, building healthy foundations for the future? Or had we blundered through, grasping at half-measures and missed chances, sowing the seeds of economic failure, social division and nuclear war?

Towards the end of 1959, after the year's events had provided plenty of food for thought, the nation was asked for answers, as Harold Macmillan's Conservatives went for a record-breaking third straight election win.

Everyman's (and many women's) passport to personal freedom, and arguably the design of the decade – the Mini changed the face, and the price, of popular motoring.

What Do You Want (If You Don't Want Money)?

Adam Faith didn't ask until after the election, but Labour had been offering alternatives to simple materialism for years. Fairer distribution of wealth and scaled-down defence commitments were the current options, and Gaitskell's party argued that the gap between rich and poor was growing. It made no attempt to deny that almost everyone was a lot better off than they had been in 1951, when the Tories came to power.

Unemployment and inflation were issues, but not the economic monsters they would become: about 400,000 were out of work by the autumn and the cost of living had gone up by about ten percent over the decade. Meanwhile, a working- man's average weekly wage had almost doubled to reach £11. 2s. 6d (£11.12), and that year's budget was the seventh in a row to feature basic tax cuts.

Five million over-16s were still too young to vote or draw the dole, but four million had jobs. With the end of conscription fixed for next year, the issue of providing them with leisure facilities figured in all the party manifestos, another sign that lifestyle expectations had come a long way. The air was getting cleaner, oil had just been discovered in the North Sea, and even the Third World War was looking a little less likely – with hard work and good luck, people could hope to do more than just get by.

Less than three in ten families owned their homes, but some 750,000 first-time buyers had entered the market since 1951, as new housing steadily replaced slums and bomb sites. Labour counted three million homes without their own plumbed toilet, but more than two thirds of all households had television, a third had washing machines and, perhaps most importantly, one in three had their own motorised transport.

Slow Lanes

By now, half a million new cars per year were being sold in Britain. A lot of people, especially in the more prosperous south, were getting used to visiting the seaside, friends or relatives in their cars, or even driving to work. What they lacked were good roads.

It's Day One on the brand new M1 near Luton, but it looks as if most people are still stuck on the North Circular.

On 2 November the Transport Minister Ernest Marples opened the first 72-mile stretch of the M1 motorway. Linking London and Birmingham, it was Britain's first motorway – apart from a seven-mile segment of the Preston by-pass – but it arrived to criticism from all sides. Some critics claimed that motorways would make town congestion worse, others that they took the pleasure out of driving, but the main complaint was that they were taking so long to arrive.

Germany's Autobahns had been famous before the War, but Britain didn't begin planning motorways until 1947. A national numbering system had been announced and six numbered roads had since been drawn on maps, but the other five were still notional or barely under construction, and the M1's extension into Yorkshire was already well overdue. At a time when roads were seen as crucial to social and economic growth, British motorists were still stuck with a network of elderly trunk roads connecting jammed-up towns.

Box Bursts Bubble

In August 1959 the BMC Mini, known either as the Morris Mini or the Austin Seven, was launched. British motoring would never be quite the same again.

BMC's chief designer, Sir Alec Issigonis, had produced a car that was compact enough for modern city use, cheap enough for genuine mass appeal, able to carry four adults, and, crucially, an instant style hit. It had taken every trick in the book to achieve it – putting the 850cc engine in sideways to save space, and stripping away all unnecessary detail, inside and out – but the result was a success story that rolled on for almost half a century, including a starring role in the Swinging Sixties and more than 5 million worldwide sales.

The Mini liberated a lot of young drivers, but it dealt a serious blow to Britain's two-wheeled trade and killed off one of the decade's most endearing fads, the bubble car. Originally imported from Germany, bubble cars brought hair-raising names such as Heinkel and Messerschmidt to Britain's streets in the 50s, along with classier models such as the BMW Isetta. They were cheap, cheeky, could be driven on a bike licence and boasted miserly fuel consumption, a particularly important consideration in the aftermath of Suez. Fuel was more plentiful by 1959, and cheaper tax hardly mattered when a bubble car cost around £650 and a new Mini was only £425. At the other end of the scale, you could buy 20 Minis, and have six months' wages left, for the price of another British motoring institution, the Rolls Royce Phantom V .

Death On Wheels

More cars on poor roads meant more accidents, particularly before 70 mph speed limits, and road safety would be a small but sharp election issue. On 22 January, the dangers of speeding were highlighted when Britain's first Formula One world champion, Mike Hawthorn, died when he crashed his Jaguar at 100 mph on the Guildford by-pass.

Grand Prix racing was something of a national obsession, especially since the

Stirling Moss in his car at Silverstone during the British Grand Prix. Everything about Moss was as British as they come, from his name, his upright demeanour and his racing green Jaguar, right down to his habit of nearly, but not quite, winning world championships.

gripping world championship of 1958. In the absence of the retired Fangio, it was fought out between two British drivers, Mike Hawthorn and Stirling Moss. The upright, dashing Moss drove in the racing green of Britain's Vanwall cars, and was probably the popular favourite. Hawthorn had spent years driving Jaguars, but was behind the wheel of a Ferrari when he clinched the title at Casablanca in the final race.

The races, and circuits, were extremely dangerous. Hawthorn's team-mates Luigi Musso and Peter Collins, winner of the Silverstone Grand Prix, were both killed during the 1958 season, and British driver Stuart Lewis-Evans had died after his Vanwall caught fire. The irony of Hawthorn's death, a few months after he had retired as champion, touched a public chord, and thousands filed past the crash site to pay tribute over the next few days.

The Adventures of Nikita, Part Two

In February, Harold Macmillan became the first Western leader to visit the Soviet Union in peacetime. The visit was fraught with snubs and demonstrations of Britain's reduced importance, but it did help sort out the latest Berlin crisis and left 'Supermac' with a not unfavourable view of Khrushchev, who he called 'a mixture of Peter the Great and Lord Beaverbrook'.

In July, when Richard Nixon visited Moscow, Khrushchev took the chance to make an impression on America. A televised debate was arranged at an American exhibition in the city – in a kitchen exhibit – and the Soviet premier engaged Nixon in a carefully orchestrated chat about capitalism, Communism and consumerism. These were just Khrushchev's warm-up performances. The big show came in mid-September when, at Eisenhower's invitation, he and his wife arrived in the United States for a two-week visit.

The trip held the world's attention, but wasn't a complete success. Khrushchev's hosts did their best to impress him with their wealth, and he encountered a lot of rudeness from Commie-haters, particularly during a stressful tour of Los Angeles, where he caught the rough end of Gary Cooper's patriotic tongue. Khrushchev's appearance at the United Nations and a set of superficial talks at Camp David both passed off

Ernesto 'Che' Guevara was from Argentina, and played an important part in the Cuban revolution. Seen here settling into his role as economic advisor to Fidel Castro's new regime, he would later fight and die for revolution in Bolivia. None of which explains why he ended up as the world's most famous wall poster.

cordially, and the Soviet premier sailed through it all with stoic good humour, just as he had done in Britain four years earlier.

Nothing concrete had been achieved, but Khrushchev was talking again and John Foster Dulles was gone, killed by cancer in May. As the decade ended, the 'spirit of Camp David' and the prospect of a new president in 1960 revived hopes that the worst of the Cold War was over.

No Cigar

One legacy of the Dulles era had disappeared, never to return. In Cuba, the bloodthirsty Batista regime had fallen to Fidel Castro's small band of nationalist rebels, which had taken power in Havana on New Year's Day. With Dulles still in office, the United States had reacted by branding Castro a Communist and threatening sanctions against Cuban sugar. Castro responded by nationalising the sugar industry, and the mould was cast. Pushed into dependence on Soviet aid, Castro developed his regime into a hybrid brand of Communism, while Washington tried everything imaginable to rid itself of the menace on its doorstep, from sabotaging Castro's beard and cigars to training an army of exiles for a counter-invasion. It was a mess, and it would soon turn very dangerous.

Prime Minister Harold Macmillan turns on the charm during a Downing Street chat with President Eisenhower. Ike, due to meet Khrushchev in the next few weeks and only a few months from retirement, ponders a putt.

Family Gathering

Crown and governments had spent the decade promoting the Commonwealth as a natural development of Empire. There had been a few violent hiccups along the way, but in 1959 it was deemed appropriate to officially rename Empire Day, and 24 May became Commonwealth Day. By now the Commonwealth included some 600 million citizens of independent states, and further decolonisation was accepted British policy, with Nigeria and the West Indies next on the agenda. The process of transformation was still beset with problems – Aden was a war zone, racial tension in Rhodesia refused to stabilise, Cyprus was only just settling down and several African countries appeared ripe for civil war – but on the whole the experiment seemed to be working. Hopes that the Commonwealth would maintain Britain in a cocoon of preferential trade arrangements were to be dashed within a few years, but it has survived as a valuable alternative forum for international debate and policy-making.

The Clan Macmillan

Deep into his third year at Number 10, Harold Macmillan was an undoubted asset to his party's election campaign. In government since 1951 – as housing minister, defence minister and Chancellor – he had never quite allowed his reassuring old-world charm to conceal a sharp, calculating mind, and he was a shrewd manipulator behind the scenes. A confident and graceful public performer, he enjoyed a friendly relationship with the Queen but was also one of the first politicians to make television viewers feel as if they were listening to a real person. Macmillan was in many ways a modern statesman, with an ear open to public opinion and an eye on new horizons, but his cabinet was also a last echo of the aristocratic age. Supermac himself was married to a daughter of the Duke of Devonshire and his colleagues included three family members, along with a duke, a marquess and four earls.

Rag Trade

It was feared that television would kill off reading for pleasure, but though 60 percent of adults were already watching between three and five hours of TV every night the opposite had turned out to be true.

Book sales doubled in the 50s, and even the country's world-beating intake of newspapers grew a little. A few papers, such as the *News Chronicle*, were struggling to survive, and circulation champion the *News of the World* had been pegged back from 8 million to 6.7 million readers, but the 'popular' press, the Sundays and the 'quality' dailies were all doing well. Just over a quarter of a million people read *The Times* every day, and the *Manchester Guardian*'s rising circulation, approaching 190,000, had just persuaded it to drop the city from its title and consider itself a national daily.

Television did more damage to evening papers, which went into permanent decline, and ITV's appetite for advertising starved many illustrated weeklies to death. *Picture Post*, *Illustrated* and *Everyman* had all closed down in 1957, despite having sold a million copies per week between them in 1950. Well-known *Picture Post* reporters such as Kenneth Allsop, Alan Whicker, Trevor Philpott and Fyfe Robertson became television journalists.

Crowds in Valetta, enraged by closure of the naval dockyards and the arrest of nationalist leaders, demand independence for Malta. Withdrawal from Malta, regarded as a strategically vital military base, wasn't one of the Empire's success stories, and the island suffered years of civil unrest before it won independence in 1964.

How Was It For You?

No election was necessary until next year, but Macmillan went to the nation while the economy was healthy. The government bolstered its position with a popular budget, hired an advertising agency and set polling day for 8 October. The election's defining phrase was uttered by the PM in Bedford, where he told voters, 'you've never had it so good'. He then hedged the claim with a series of qualifications, none of which had quite the same impact.

The campaign was more lively than the last, and a seven percent Tory lead soon began to slip. Macmillan had done well to maintain a united cabinet during a stormy parliament, but Labour had also been healing its internal rifts. Gaitskell had managed to get Nye Bevan back into the shadow cabinet, and the party's appeal to moral values over personal greed seemed to be making headway. Gaitskell was never able to match Macmillan's statesmanlike demeanour, but precedent suggested the country would vote for change, and by election day pollsters were predicting a desperately close race.

They didn't get one. An increased turnout saw the Conservatives enter the new parliament with 365 MPs, including newcomer Margaret Thatcher, and a majority of 100 seats. Gaitskell remained in charge of a shocked Labour Party, amid doubts that it could ever challenge for power again, while the Liberals remained stuck on six, despite a modestly successful campaign by well-liked leader Jo Grimmond.

So Britain settled down to the decade's last winter with a declared sense that the world was getting better. More people than ever enjoyed property, comfort and the pursuit of pleasures. A generation of teenagers was about to enter adulthood with expectations their parents would have laughed at; and the very young would grow up to inhabit a world of almost unlimited opportunity and plenty. That, at least, was the outlook endorsed by the landslide of 1959.

Eamonn Andrews gives his mum a cuddle. The former insurance clerk and Irish middleweight champion was perhaps *the* voice of 50s Britain. A full-time BBC sports commentator from 1950, he went on to host radio programmes, voiceover newsreels and present TV shows, including *This Is Your Life.*

OTHER NEWS...

... De Gaulle is elected French president in January... Henry Cooper lifts British and European heavyweight titles by defeating Brian London... Buddy Holly, Ritchie Valens and JP "The Big Bopper" Richardson die in Iowa plane crash on 3 February... 18 March, Macmillan and Eisenhower meet in Ottawa... *Ben-Hur* wins best film Oscar, and is the third highest earner of the decade... best actor goes to Charlton Heston, Simone Signoret is best actress... the Chinese conquer Tibet, after an uprising in March, and force the Dalai Lama to flee... Nottingham Forest beat Luton Town 2-1 in the Cup final.. Wolves win their second consecutive league title... Rangers and St Mirren take Scots honours... Singapore becomes self-governing on 3 June... the St Lawrence Seaway opens... *Juke Box Jury* is first shown in June... *The Naked Lunch* by William Burroughs ...US record sales reach $600 million... spy Klaus Fuchs is released from prison and flies to East Berlin... Obscene Publications Act comes into effect... Hawaii becomes the 50th state of the USA... royal pregnancy announced in August... Barbie dolls arrive... Scotland's first nuclear power station opens at Chapelcross, Dumfries... Robert A Heinlein publishes *Starship Troopers*.... ICI and Shell CEOs earn about £50,000 pa, the PM earns £10,000 pa, and the Queen receives a total of £475,000 from the state... in September, the Queen makes the first STD call, to the Lord Provost in Edinburgh... postcodes are introduced in November... 15% of US households now own two cars... the Marriage Guidance Council now has 18,000 clients... *Billy Liar* from Keith Waterhouse... satirist Tom Lehrer's albums released in Britain... *Savannah* is the world's first nuclear-powered surface ship... only 0.1% of black American children study with whites... civil war underway in Vietnam... London negotiations end civil war in Cyprus, which will have a Greek president and a Turkish vice-president.... Anglia, Tyne Tees and Ulster Television begin broadcasting... goodbye: Raymond Chandler, Lou Costello, Cecil B. DeMille, Errol Flynn, Gilbert Harding, Mike Hawthorn, Lord Halifax, Billie Holiday, George Marshall, Frank Lloyd Wright...

Epilogue

The electorate that showed such faith in the future had been both right and wrong. Much of the material promise of the 50s has been fulfilled, especially where communications and standards of living are concerned. The world is our oyster, and millions of us enjoy lifestyles beyond even the dreams of Norah Docker. On the other hand, easy living and the world at our fingertips haven't exactly made us happy.

The nation's economic condition, its social cohesion and its place in the world have all plumbed depths unimaginable to Macmillan's audiences, while the business of wealth generation has traded away innocence from art, music and sport. The communications revolution has turned fashion into a word for 'fifteen minutes', made a new world power of mass media, and helped splinter what was once a relatively straightforward cultural identity into millions of fragments.

The planet as a whole has made equally mixed progress. The United Nations is still in place, the Cold War eventually ended without boiling over, and no decade has ever played fast and loose with atomic energy quite like the 50s. Then again, nuclear weapons haven't gone away, there may be no way to get rid of nuclear reactors, and nobody's pretending the world has found peaceful plenty.

When Harold Macmillan opened the new decade by talking of a 'wind of change blowing through Africa', he was behind the times and missing the point. Decolonisation was effectively over, while the seeds of massive economic, health and environmental crises were sprouting unattended. Third World poverty, disease and political instability were all global problems in the 50s, but are bigger ones today, fighting for attention alongside new menaces such as AIDS and ecological degradation.

Is modern life better, or worse, than when Britain voted for more of the same in 1959? Could a different path through the preceding decade have prevented racial violence, social division or global poverty, let alone global warming, road congestion and all the other environmental side-effects of post-War economic growth? The jury will be out for a long time to come, and looking back may never provide full answers, but it is difficult to reach any conclusions about today's world without at least a glance back at the 50s.